What **Coco Chanel** Can Teach **You** About **Fashion**

FRANCES LINCOLN

Caroline Young

Contents

04	Introduction
138	Glossary
141	Picture Credits
142	Index

The Inspiration

52	Don't Forget your Past
56	Embrace your Social Circle
60	Use your Own Image
62	Speak the Language of Revolution
66	Choose Love as an Influence
70	Express your Artistic Temperament
72	Arouse the Trailblazers
76	Harness the Dramatic
80	Look to your Location
84	Feel the Heat
88	Appeal to the Hot New Thing
92	Rebel Against your Rivals

The Looks

10	Combine the Masculine and the Feminine
14	Simplicity can be Luxury
18	Embrace the Zeitgeist
20	Keep it Simple with Black
24	Explore Innovations that Endure
28	Find Luxury in White Satin
32	Escape Reality with Romance
34	Make a Statement with Monochrome
36	Refine your Colour Palette
40	Source Quality Fabric
42	Don't Forget the Accessories
46	Play with Past Successes

The Details

96	Twist Textile Traditions
100	Choose a Fabric with Durability
104	Find Magic in Numbers
106	Embellish with Embroidery
110	Say it with Stripes
114	See it in the Stars
118	Expose New Parts of the Body
122	Faux Jewellery can be Priceless
124	Don't Shy from the Glitz
128	Discover your Own Motif
132	Find your Spirit Animal
134	Create a Timeless Signature Accessory

Introduction

As the original fashion rebel of the early twentieth century, Gabrielle 'Coco' Chanel's individual attitude and essence shaped her ground-breaking designs. Her timeless style offered both luxury and comfort with simple lines, soft tailoring, touches of romantic embellishment and a predominantly black, white and beige colour scheme. And they also revealed the secrets about her life and loves.

1883	1895	1910	1913	1921	1926	1939	1954	1971
Gabrielle Chanel is born in Saumur, France.	Chanel arrives at Aubazine Abbey.	Opens her first shop, Chanel, Modes, on rue Cambon, Paris.	Opens her Deauville boutique.	The launch of Chanel Nº5.	Chanel's Little Black Dress is featured in *Vogue*.	Chanel closes down her business.	Chanel makes her comeback.	Chanel dies at The Ritz, Paris.

Disregarding the Rules

Born into poverty and raised in a convent, Coco Chanel set her own rules on how to live. Through her creativity, she freed women from the corset and played with gendered dress, using items from male wardrobes and adapting them for a female silhouette. With her short hair, tanned skin and love affairs, in which she disregarded the rules, she was symbolic of the modern, freedom-loving woman of the 1920s, as represented by her boyish *garçonne* look. In the 1950s, following the designer's post-war comeback, Chanel considered clothing for the active, independent woman – breaking from the nipped-in Dior 'New Look' – with dresses and suits that allowed women to breathe.

Her designs attracted the most fashionable women in the world – society ladies and courtesans, Parisian stage actresses, stylish British aristocrats and cinema icons. Her collections over the years changed little – the tweed jacket, the Little Black Dress, ropes of pearls, Breton tops, the quilted bags, a splash of Chanel Nº5 – all still considered status symbols for the chic, modern woman. She was the perfect model for her own clothes, and the fabrics, silhouettes and motifs she chose, including the number five, the lion symbol and the camellia, all spoke a secret code.

The Endurance of Style

Such is the potency of Coco Chanel, that even after her death, the House of Chanel consistently referenced the past, using the fashion vocabulary that she pioneered. She was a self-taught couturiere who fought for independence so she could live her life the way she wanted. Chanel created an eternal style to inspire women, fulfilling their need for a comfortable uniform for modern life. As Chanel once said: 'Fashion changes but style endures.'

To help understand what defines Coco Chanel, this book sets out the lessons we can learn from her, breaking down the key looks, her inspiration and the anatomy of her designs. Each lesson helps to uncover Chanel's creative spirit, revealing how we can apply her rules and lessons today in fashion, attitude and style. So celebrate the artistry behind Chanel, delve into her innovative approach and her rebellious attitude, and learn how to look at fashion in a new light.

Coco Chanel's Legacy

Gabrielle Chanel was born in Saumur, in the Loire Valley, France, on 19 August 1883. Her travelling salesman father moved Chanel and her four siblings from town to town as he sold garments from his cart. This impoverished childhood shaped her life and career. Chanel was twelve when her mother died; she and her two sisters were taken to the remote convent at Aubazine Abbey, in the Corrèze region of France, where they were raised by nuns. This experience influenced what was to become the classic Chanel style – the use of monochrome, her simple and austere designs, the symbols from the sun and moon mosaics in the corridors of the convent, the number five embodied within the Cistercian abbey and the double C logo from the patterns in its windows.

The Emergence of Coco

At the age of eighteen, Chanel moved to the town of Moulins to work as a seamstress with her aunt, Antoinette. In the evenings, she sang at the town's rowdy café-concerts which were frequented by the men of the Tenth Light Horse regiment. One of these dashing young men was Étienne Balsan. From a wealthy textile family, Balsan had come into an inheritance after his parents died. He had an unconventional outlook and became enamoured by the poor, orphaned Chanel. He nicknamed her 'Coco', said to come from a popular ditty that she sang as part of her repertoire – *Qui qu'a vu Coco*.

Balsan's first love was horse racing and he left the army to live at Royallieu, his converted château outside Paris, where his frequent guests included members of high society and the courtesans of the demimonde. Chanel followed him there, and she was absorbed into the carefree lifestyle of this country estate – riding horses in the forests and going to watch the horse racing at famous tracks like Longchamps.

She spoke with disdain of the clothes the women wore to the races, with their 'enormous loaves on their heads, constructions made of feathers and improved with fruits and plumes', observing that 'worst of all, which appalled me,

their hats did not fit on their heads'. Chanel, with her gamine looks, stood out in the way she chose to dress, in tailored riding jackets, jodhpurs and simple little straw hats. When actress and courtesan Émilienne d'Alençon wore one of Chanel's straw boaters embellished by the designer, it immediately attracted attention, and soon Chanel had a list of clients all wanting their own little boyish hats.

Establishing a Brand

Chanel's designs were much sought after by fashionable Parisian women, and with the help of rich English playboy Arthur 'Boy' Capel, she established a hat business. The cocottes dressed to attract men, and so by stripping back the embellishments, Chanel was taking away their dependence. Boy encouraged Chanel to open a shops in Paris and Deauville in 1913, and her designs quickly earned a following amongst aristocrats, artists and actresses. Her use of jersey was completely novel. Soon her designs captured the zeitgeist of the First World War, and society women in Paris visited her studio to be fitted with simple but luxurious clothing that gave them a touch of the Coco Chanel magic. Her loose-fitting blouses with pockets and low waistlines helped free women from tight, restrictive corsets, and by the 1920s they all wished to dress like Chanel. Boy Capel is thought to have been the love of Chanel's life. He was tragically killed in a car accident just before Christmas 1919 and Chanel later lamented that 'in losing

Boy, I lost everything'. His death was a huge blow to her, and she sought to prove her own worth by building up an empire, which included best-selling perfumes.

Chanel was at the forefront of fashion in the 1920s, mixing in a bohemian circle which included artist's muse Misia Sert, Pablo Picasso, Igor Stravinsky, Jean Cocteau and Sergei Diaghilev, founder of the Ballets Russes. The places she visited shaped her designs – she gleaned tweeds from Scotland when travelling with her lover, the Duke of Westminster, Breton tops from her time in Deauville, white pyjamas and Navy insignia from yachting in the South of France.

Throughout her career she favoured a black, white and beige colour scheme, inspired by the palette of the remote Aubazine Abbey where she was raised. But she also used touches of romance from the Belle Époque, the drama of the baroque and the influence of the Russian émigrés in Paris in the 1920s, as is evident in her embroidery and the tulle, lace and sequin details on her gowns. These feminine, romantic touches contrasted with the simplicity of the LBD (the Little Black Dress) designed to be essential and discreet.

Stylish Clothes for the Modern World

In 1939, on the outbreak of the Second World War, Chanel closed down her fashion house and retreated to Switzerland, where she lived in semi-exile for almost ten years.

Yet she emerged in the 1950s to reign over fashion with her classic tweed suit. It initially caught on with American women who admired the freedom it gave them, and soon swept the world as an essential element in the active woman's wardrobe. The new women of the 1950s and 60s who evoked the Chanel spirit included Brigitte Bardot, Suzy Parker, Jeanne Moreau and Jackie Kennedy.

Coco Chanel continued to create collections that followed her favoured aesthetic right up to her death in January 1971, at the age of eighty-seven. She had been living at the Ritz in Paris since the 1930s, which looked onto her workrooms and salon at 31 Rue Cambon. Her legacy carried on after her death, with Rue Cambon continuing to be her spiritual home.

Karl Lagerfeld was appointed head of Chanel in 1983. He redefined the Chanel look, using classic touches while incorporating a sense of fun. He raked the archives to find inspiration, yet also pushed boundaries with candy coloured tweed suits, the Chanel logo printed onto textiles and in jewellery, a giant hula-hoop quilted bag and microscopic monochrome bikinis. As Lagerfeld once said: 'My job is not to do what she did but what she would have done. The good thing about Chanel is it is an idea you can adapt to many things.'

On his death in 2019, Lagerfeld was succeeded by Virginie Viard, who continues to tell the life story of Chanel through the language of the past, while also following Chanel's ethos of creating wearable, comfortable clothing for the present and the future.

The
Looks

Combine the **Masculine** and the **Feminine**

When it came to developing her classic style, Coco Chanel was shaped by the wardrobe of the men in her life — a polo sweater borrowed from Arthur 'Boy' Capel, a quilted jacket from the stable boys at Royallieu, a tweed sporting jacket from the Duke of Westminster. When she first emerged as a designer in the 1910s, fashions were ultra-feminine. All bosoms and hips, women were synched into an s-shape, with heavy corsetry under extravagant lace gowns and over-embellished hats balancing precariously on their heads. Combining masculine touches with a feminine aesthetic, Chanel turned fashion on its head.

→ Kate Moss modelling the Chanel spring 1994 ready-to-wear collection, demonstrating the slouchy masculine style that Coco Chanel originally forged in the 1910s.

During her days at Étienne Balsan's Château de Royallieu, Chanel spent her time galloping through the surrounding forests on horseback. Inspired by the jockeys and stable lads, she was the tomboy in jodhpurs, a blouse with tie and a custom-made tweed jacket. For their regular fancy dress parties, she was known to wear a man's suit with ease, and this would also shape her love of masculine style in the last days of the Belle Époque era.

The lives of women changed dramatically during the First World War, including in the way they dressed. As they contributed to the war effort by working in factories or driving ambulances, they required looser, less cumbersome clothing. Chanel's simple, practical designs with masculine touches, originally sold from her boutique in Deauville in Normandy, immediately captured this movement. Her chemises featured v-necks with buttons down the front, as in a man's sweater, and a loose sash slung low at the waist. Women's clothing typically didn't have

↑   Society girl and model Marisa
Berenson pictured in *Vogue*
1969, wearing Chanel's tunic and
culottes, inspired by the hippie
subculture that looked east.

"What was needed was simplicity, comfort, neatness: unwittingly I offered all of that."

Chanel

pockets, but Chanel insisted on this feature in her tunics to free up hands. Instead of being restricted, it brought women freedom in their clothing. 'I was in the right place, an opportunity beckoned. I took it … What was needed was simplicity, comfort, neatness: unwittingly I offered all of that.'

Chanel, like style icons Marlene Dietrich and Katharine Hepburn, was a trailblazer in championing trousers for women in the 1920s and 1930s, at a time when they were considered quite scandalous for women to wear. Chanel's gleaming white satin pyjamas, first worn by the designer around 1918, and her wide trousers worn with a striped

top, were for easy days on the Riviera or for glamorous evenings when worn with a matching jacket.

In the 1960s, Chanel created evening trouser suits with spaghetti strap tops in embroidered silk and metallic tweeds, rivalling the cutting-edge Le Smoking suits by Yves Saint Laurent. A staunch opponent of the mini skirt, Chanel's compromise to this youthful trend was the culotte suit – Bermuda-style shorts with a tunic over the top, which was in tune with the Eastern-inspired bohemian subcultures.

Simplicity can be **Luxury**

'Some people think luxury is the opposite of poverty. It is not. It is the opposite of vulgarity,' Chanel once said.

In a style that became known as '*genre pauvre*', or '*poverty de luxe*', Chanel took items that were originally considered working class and marketed them, with a high price tag, to high society women. In her collections, Chanel adopted the pocketed jackets of a working man, the black-and-white uniform of a housemaid or a Breton fisherman's striped top, and she was revolutionary in utilising 'poor' fabrics like flannel and jersey, which tended to be used for men's underwear.

→ Coco Chanel modelling her collection of comfortable jersey pieces at Étretat beach, near Deauville, in 1913. The loose jacket featured deep pockets and a slouchy belt with camellia detail.

Before the First World War, affluent women squeezed themselves into restrictive, uncomfortable clothing, as it was a signifier of their status. But Chanel's exclusive designs removed all the trappings of wealth, such as crinolines and bustles, restrictive corsets and boned bodices. It was the daring woman who stripped away the ostentatious displays of heavy lace, feathers and jewels, instead replacing them with the simple — a jersey chemise or one of Chanel's straw boater hats.

Chanel broke into fashion at the right time, as her style suited the aesthetics of the First World War, when a shortage of fabric and metal led to a drive for more austere clothing. She was quick to adapt, incorporating cheaper rabbit fur trimmings instead of expensive sable and mink, and using jersey in a ground-breaking way. *Vogue* wrote of how both the war and jersey occupied the minds of fashionable Parisians, and that 'jersey is no longer a fabric, it is an obsession'.

14

"Jersey is no longer a fabric, it's an obsession"

Vogue

Even after the war, Chanel continued to use jersey for her range of separates consisting of sweaters, skirts and cardigans, and simple black outfits with contrasting white collars and cuffs. She elevated working-class style into luxury, with fine tailoring and uncompromising technique. In an article in 1931, American journalist Janet Flanner described how Chanel looked to 'the ditch-digger's scarf, made chic the white collars and cuffs of the waitress, and put queens into mechanics' tunics'.

Chanel's *genre pauvre* clothing democratised fashion, as her simple designs were transferred onto the streets when women across Europe and the United States copied the style for themselves. Chanel said 'a fine fabric is beautiful in itself, but the more lavish a dress is, the poorer it becomes. People confused poverty with simplicity.'

← A revisionist design of Chanel's ground-breaking Deauville look, with a cardigan jacket with deep pockets, a blouse, and straw boater hat, from spring-summer 1989.

Embrace
the Zeitgeist

In the 1920s, Chanel earned her reputation as a fashion vanguard. Paris was a city for bohemians, of new cutting-edge art movements such as Cubism, Futurism and Art Deco. By immersing herself in new trends and collaborating with brilliant people, Chanel would maintain her position at the forefront of the zeitgeist. As well as energising the flapper and embracing the sportswear look, she was one of the first women in Paris to cut her hair boyishly short, of which she said, 'everyone went into raptures'.

Chanel built on the success she found during the First World War, as her elegant yet comfortable designs appealed to women who wished to maintain their newfound freedoms in peacetime. As well as her coats with big pockets, Chanel created looser skirts so women could step easily onto Paris's underground system, Le Métropolitan. The straight silhouette of the 1920s became known in France as the 'garçonne' look, after the controversial novel by Victor Margueritte. It was defined by Chanel's pleated skirts, sweaters and fluid dresses, which skimmed the body and were shaped to be worn without a corset.

Chanel was aware that her customers were modern, 'busy women' and there was a Chanel outfit for all activities, from playing tennis and golf, to going to dinner at the casino or watching horse racing. 'A dress made right should allow one to walk, to dance, even to ride horseback!' she said. As a fashion leader, her designs came to represent the free-thinking woman who cropped her hair, shimmered in knee-length, skin-exposing gowns and spritzed herself with the new scent of that era, Chanel N°5.

→ Chanel looked to the 1925 International Exhibition of Modern Decorative and Industrial Arts, where Art Deco was born. This launched Paris as the centre of cutting-edge art and design, and pulsating jazz. Chanel's 1925 collection played up to the Eastern-inspired motifs that defined Art Deco, while incorporating jersey and jazzy knee-length skirts. Throughout the 1920s, skirt lengths were raised and dropped, but Chanel chose to keep the hem just below the knee, which suited the new generation of active, modern women who tanned their skin and learned new energetic dances.

Keep it **Simple** with **Black**

It was in 1926 that Chanel officially launched her Little Black Dress, an item that would become the easy wardrobe essential for women, inspiring everyone from Louise Brooks to Holly Golightly in the movie *Breakfast at Tiffany's*. It would be known simply as the LBD.

Made from black crepe de Chine, Chanel's dress was an elegant sheath with long sleeves and was worn with a string of gleaming pearls. It was 'little' because it was discreet, and it was immediately hailed by American *Vogue* as the equivalent of the Ford motor car, as they foresaw it becoming an everyday essential.

→ Just as Coco Chanel in 1918 earned plaudits for a black sheath surrounded by a black tulle crinoline, Karl Lagerfeld created an updated version for his autumn-winter 1991–92 collection.

It was not the first time Chanel had used black — she first created loose v-necked black gowns in 1917 from jersey enriched with silk, decorated with Japanese embroidery. She also earned plaudits for a series of black gowns in 1918, including a crepe de Chine sheath surrounded by a black tulle crinoline, and a black gown with thin straps and a peplum at the hips.

Chanel's early black gowns were in velvet, georgette chiffon and mousseline, with black silk fringing or chiffon flowers, and while it was thought the colour erased the shape of a woman's body, it suited the Art Deco aesthetic of the 1920s, where minimalism was the ultimate in chic elegance. 'Black is the smartest of colours for evening,' wrote *Vogue* in 1926.

Despite it traditionally being for mourning, black, according to Chanel, was a colour that could transition from day to night, from wool to silk crepe, satin and velvet. Chanel claimed she was hit by a desire for women to wear black when she saw all the garishly

"Black is the smartest of colours for evening."

Vogue

colourful Paul Poiret gowns at a charity ball in Paris in 1920. She said those colours were 'impossible' in their wearability and that 'black wipes out everything else around'.

The simplicity of the Little Black Dress acted as a canvas for strings of pearls, jewelled belts and contrasting white collars and cuffs. 'For four of five years I made only black. My dresses sold like mad with little touches – a white collar, or cuffs. Everyone wore them – actresses, society women, housemaids.'

Chanel continued to incorporate black following her comeback in the 1950s. For her 1954 collection, she created a black velvet shirt-waist evening gown with a full skirt and black lace strapless gowns. Black would remain a classic for Chanel – a reliable favourite that defined her brand.

Explore Innovations
that Endure

'**I make fashions women can live in, breathe** in, feel comfortable in, and look young in,' Chanel once told *Vogue* fashion editor Bettina Ballard. Chanel's designs were revolutionary, as she understood exactly what women needed to feel confident.

When she launched her comeback collection in 1954, she stated that her primary motivation was to provide women with wearable clothes. The most popular piece in the collection became known as The Chanel Look and featured a jacket with easy pockets, a mid-calf skirt, sleek blouse and straw boater. It personified casual elegance, and in the way it was constructed, the wearer could not help but take a youthful and chic stance, with the hips pushed forward and with one hand in the pocket.

The tweet jacket quickly became a signature of Chanel, and with its straight silhouette and the cut of a man's jacket, it acted as a uniform for the modern woman that offered perfect freedom. Compared with the restrictive fashions of the 1950s, which followed the cinched in, waspish waist of Christian Dior's New Look, it was a style that allowed women to breathe.

These jackets may have seemed simple, yet the construction was intensive, taking 150 hours of labour to make each one, and they followed an innovative formula. Chanel developed a special cut on the shoulders so that the jacket fitted like a cardigan. There was a ribbon stitched to the waistband of the skirt to secure it to the blouse, a chain concealed in the hem to weigh it down and ensure the jacket sat well, and embossed gilt buttons, which often featured her favored symbols of the lion, to represent her Leo star sign, her signature flower, the camellia, and the interlocking Cs of the Coco Chanel logo. These motifs would be referred to time and again in Chanel's collections because of their significance in her life.

She insisted that a lining, often in silk and matching the blouse worn underneath, was a vital part of the jacket. As well as feeling luxurious, it helped the garment fall in the

↑ In 1961, *Life* magazine featured a fashion spread on the Chanel look, demonstrating how her tweed suits were the crucial style for the active woman who wanted to move about the city with ease.

→ French model Audrey Marnay at the spring-summer 2003 ready-to-wear show, wearing a tweed jacket with camellia corsage and piles of chain jewellery. The Chanel tweed jacket continued to be reinvented by Karl Lagerfeld, as he teamed it with micro-minis.

↘ Japanese music duo Amiaya wearing Chanel during Paris Fashion Week in March 2019. The Chanel tweed jacket was brought up to date as a part of the eclectic street style culture in Tokyo.

right way. 'Linings — there's the secret: linings and cut,' she said.

Chanel was unrelenting in her dedication to creating the perfect silhouette and was known to berate her seamstresses until they achieved exactly what she was after. 'I make my dresses like a watch,' she said. 'If one tiny little wheel doesn't work, I remake the dress. A dress isn't right if it is uncomfortable, if it doesn't "walk" properly ... elegance in clothes means being able to move freely, to do anything with ease.'

When Karl Lagerfeld became head of the brand in 1983, he resurrected the signature tweed jacket. While he added a modern twist to the jacket for each collection, he kept the vital pieces of Chanel's 'watch', with the hidden chain in the seam, the contrasting trim and the silk linings.

"I make my dresses like a watch... If one tiny little wheel doesn't work, I remake the dress."

Chanel

Find **Luxury** in **White Satin**

Coco Chanel saw the power of white satin. White for Chanel represented purity and cleanliness. It reminded her of the freshly laundered sheets and white petticoats at the convent where she was raised, and of the white trousseaux she had laboriously stitched as a young seamstress there.

A voracious reader of Gothic novels like *Wuthering Heights* — and embracing the image of the ghost of Cathy in her white wedding dress — Chanel's also saw white as the colour of youth and of seduction.

In 1920, she was photographed with Grand Duke Dmitri Palovich, hair cropped short and tanned skin set off beautifully by a white satin dress; the very image of gleaming modernity, and of seduction. *Vogue*, in 1923, described Chanel, 'dressed entirely in white,

and covered in pearls', highlighting how she was among the most fashionable women on the society pages.

Following the 1929 Wall Street Crash, when glamour and femininity were embraced as a means of escape from the hardships of the Great Depression, white satin gowns became ubiquitous. It was a return to the frivolity of the Belle Époque. Chanel described this period as 'candid innocence and white satin'.

In the early 1930s, Chanel continued this trend for seductive white satin by reintroducing her white beach pyjamas for wearing at the Venice Lido; they were an immediate hit in the pages of fashion magazines. When she created a version for Ina Claire in the Hollywood musical *The Greeks Had a Word for Them*, they were instantly championed by *Vogue*.

Chanel's 1933 all-white spring collection was highly innovative, and French *Vogue* described how Chanel, for the first time, showed all her white dresses in one sitting.

→ Chanel wearing her signature white satin pyjamas; a style she first developed at the end of the First World War.

'It was as if the place had suddenly been transformed into an orchard in Normandy.'

White, she said, should be dazzling in its purity, and 'mustn't look like whipped cream'. Chanel particularly enjoyed the way white reflected the sun, illuminating everything around it, and she relished the contrast of 'a very white earring on the lobe of a well-tanned ear'. White was the perfect complement to bronzed skin, and so it became the colour of the Riviera.

"Fashion is not something that exists in dresses only. Fashion is in the sky, in the street, fashion has to do with ideas, the way we live, what is happening."

Escape Reality
with **Romance**

While Chanel was famed for her masculine tailoring, her evening gowns offered a romantic and feminine contrast. By 1918, she was embellishing gowns with metallic lace and fringing, shimmering beading and delicate embroidery, and she earned a reputation for these light touches to her evening wear.

Following the Wall Street Crash of 1929, fashions dramatically shifted from the boyish, flat-chested *garçonne* look of the 1920s, to a more traditionally feminine silhouette. Skirt lengths dropped to six inches off the ground, the bias-cut clung to curves and the waistline was repositioned to its natural placing to enhance a woman's body. Like other couturiers, Chanel fully embraced this trend for femininity, creating floor-skimming gowns in sultry white and pale pink satin or with layers of frothy lace. In February 1930, she created two floor-length evening gowns, one black and one white, which featured a dropped hem and raised waist. For spring 1931, Chanel's pale gowns featured plenty of

tulle, velvet, lace and ribbon. These romantic dresses, while appearing to reference the Belle Époque style she remembered from her youth, were daring in incorporating elements of lingerie with their thin straps and plunging necklines.

As well as the fanciful embellishments of her evening gowns, she created slim-fitting tweed or velvet suits for the day, which continued the sense of romance by revealing the ruffled collar of a white blouse or a contrasting bow at the neck.

Colourful printed organza gowns marked her gypsy collection of 1939, which proved to be her final one before closing her business at the outbreak of the Second World War. She was praised for her garments' colourful sex appeal, which included puff-sleeved peasant blouses, flamenco-style skirts and camellia flowers pinned to shoulders: it was pure, feminine escapism.

Fashion editor Diana Vreeland once said: 'Everyone thinks of suits when they think of Chanel. That came later. If you could

have seen my clothes from Chanel in the
thirties – the *dégagé* gypsy skirts, the divine
brocades, the little boleros, the roses in
the hair, the paillettes nose veils – day and
evening. And the ribbons were so pretty.'

↑ A romantic detail from the
spring-summer 2002 haute couture
collection, reminiscent of Chanel's
designs in the 1930s, with elements
borrowed from lingerie. Yet while
they reflected fashions of the past,
such as from the Belle Époque era,
they were modernist in revealing
the inner workings of the dress.
Seams and stitching were on display,
as Chanel's technique became
a focal point for the designs.

Make a **Statement** with **Monochrome**

The most iconic colour combination for Chanel is the contrast of black and white, instantly recognisable with the logo of the interlocking Cs against a white background and first introduced in 1925. For Chanel, black and white worked in pure harmony.

The classic Chanel look is monochrome: a black or white tweed jacket with contrasting trimming and a matching blouse, a black skirt or trousers with white shirt or a black dress with a flash of white. This combination of black and white would be a predominant feature in Chanel's designs, perhaps most strikingly in the Little Black Dress worn with a gleaming string of white pearls.

Chanel's monochrome palette became so popular in the 1920s because it reflected the: streamlined design and geometrics that were key to the Art Deco movement.

→ Coco Chanel outside her Rue Cambon boutique in the 1960s. From its first inception in the 1910s, the Chanel branding featured the bold monochrome logo.

In 1926, she created a trend for asymmetrical earrings — with one black and one white pearl. Chanel also used black and white in her early interiors. In 1915, her new couture house in Biarritz was emblazoned with bold block lettering, standing out against the more traditional shop fronts. Similarly, after the death of Boy Capel in December 1919, the shutters of her villa on the outskirts of Paris were painted black in mourning.

As well as the ecclesiastical symbolism of the black and white habit of a nun, the contrast also reflected Chanel's desire to combine 'poorer' elements into her collections throughout her career. From her early days as a designer, conjuring up the image of a maid, a waitress or a nun, a simple black dress with distinct white collars and cuffs became an integral part of the Chanel look. These black-and-white dresses also bore the influence of the dandy — reminiscent of a black top hat and tails worn with a crisp white shirt.

Refine your Colour **Palette**

From the neutral beige and gold tones that reminded her of the stone walls and sacred relics of Aubazine Abbey, to the deep blood-red which symbolised strength and courage, Coco Chanel was steadfast in her use of key colours.

While jet black and pure white were the long-standing signatures of her brand, Chanel was consistently drawn to a particular range of hues that she repeated over and over again — red, rose pink, gold, beige and grey. These colour combinations were first seen in 1916, when she launched her Biarritz collection, and featured jersey frock coats, skirts and chemise in burgundy, white, beige and grey; colours which she would refer to time and again.

→ Beige was one of Chanel's key colours, which she used time and again in her collections. It was a grounded, neutral colour that offered a counterpoint to black, and was utilised in the spring-summer 2019 collection.

Grey, as the blend of black and white, created a softer monochromatic tone to enhance other colours. She used grey for dresses that were reminiscent of convent girl uniforms or for tweed coats and capes that featured bolder silk linings in contrasting colours.

Chanel embraced rose pink, creating soft and feminine jersey day dresses as part of the *garçonne* look. The pink of her tulle and lace gowns in the 1930s enhanced their light-as-air appearance and perfectly encapsulated the romantic, escapist mood of the decade — a reaction to the turmoil of the Depression and the mass unrest leading up to a new global conflict.

Gold was the perfect finishing touch, dazzling in the gilt buttons and braidings on her suits, and in the chain details she loved to incorporate. It reminded Chanel of the Byzantine treasures she saw when visiting Venice and of the baroque art she adored, and the walls of her Rue Cambon apartment even glinted gold.

"Red, it's the colour of blood and we've so much inside us it's only right to show a little outside."

Chanel

'Brown and beige are the predominant colours used by Chanel,' wrote the *New York Times* in August 1923. The warm tone of beige was a colour that came from the natural stone walls at Aubazine Abbey and the earth of the Auvergne region where it is located. The neutrality of beige also helped to act as a counterpoint to the extremes of black and white. Chanel often used beige in contrast to black, as with her two-tone shoes, first introduced in 1957, where the beige helped to elongate the leg.

In the early 1920s, both beige and red emerged as favoured colours, and sometimes they were combined to form Art Deco geometric designs. Chanel explained her preferences: 'I take refuge in beige because it's natural. Not dyed. Red, it's the colour of blood and we've so much inside us it's only right to show a little outside.'

Chanel used red for velvet coats and ruby-red flapper dresses in the 1920s, and as a luxury silk lining for her soft tweed jackets in the 1950s. As she got older, she always wore a slash of red lipstick, as she believed it acted as armour for a woman to go on the attack.

Source **Quality** Fabric

'Luxury must be comfortable, otherwise it is not luxury,' Coco Chanel said. Every textile that Chanel personally selected was chosen for how it enhanced the design. Chanel used crepe de Chine for her sumptuous gowns, with touches of lace and tulle. Her knits were infused with metallic lace and beading to give a shimmering effect, and she enriched jersey with silk to make it even more luxurious.

Jersey was Chanel's signature material from her early days as a designer, when it was a daring move to use a fabric made for men's underwear. With embroidery and careful cutting, she lifted its status, as she liked how it felt and the way it draped. In the 1920s, Chanel's signature long cardigan and sweaters, worn with pleated skirts, were

→ The right fabric was vital for Chanel, as the texture and weight worked in synergy with her design. She could tell if it was a lightweight Italian tweed, or a more robust tweed from the Scottish Borders just by touching it.

made from jersey and Fair Isle tricot; smooth on one side and textured on the other.

It was the Duke of Westminster who fired up Chanel's passion for tweed, after she met him in 1923. Sturdy hunting jackets were an important element of the British aristocratic uniform, and she borrowed the Duke's tweed jackets at his Highland estate. Inspired by their comfort and durability, she sought out good quality tweed for her own collections. 'I brought in tweeds from Scotland; home-spuns came to oust crepes and muslins,' she said. 'I asked wholesalers for natural colours; I wanted women to be guided by nature, to obey the mimicry of animals.'

Aware that making her own textiles would add an incentive for her customers, in the early 1920s, Chanel established her own textile factory, Tricots Chanel. As well as commissioning new designers, Chanel would be in control of the quality of her fabrics. She brought in tweeds from manufacturer William Linton, and teamed up with English cotton firm, Ferguson Brothers, in 1930.

Don't Forget
the Accessories

Chanel began her career as an accessories designer, creating simple hats for society ladies to wear to the races and, as she progressed to couture, she was still mindful of the importance of the finishing touches to an outfit.

The well-crafted bags and shoes she created in the 1950s would be much sought-after for their reliability. The consistency of the 2.55 bag, named after its February 1955 launch date, allowed it to become an instantly recognisable sign of good taste. It featured a chain strap, and this chain detail would carry on as a strong motif for jewellery, belts and bags at the House of Chanel.

→   Chanel frequently modelled her own accessories. In this image taken by Robert Schall in Paris in 1938, she wears a yachting cap inspired by her time on the Duke of Westminster's yacht, the *Flying Cloud*, along with her famous ropes of pearls and the white enamel Maltese cross cuffs, designed in collaboration with Fulco di Verdura.

Chanel raked the past for her beige and black shoes, which originally launched in 1957. With their low heels, Chanel's slip-on shoes were an antidote to the stiletto, and the two-tone was reminiscent of those worn by the Prince of Wales and Duke of Westminster in the 1920s.

It was in this decade that Chanel unveiled her first collection of costume jewellery, which she championed over expensive gems. During the First World War, it was considered gaudy to flaunt wealth, and while other designers like Paul Poiret used costume jewellery in their collections, it was Chanel who owned it as a chic style statement. Chanel's unconventional style allowed for wearing piles of jewellery with a cardigan and skirt during the day, or even aboard a yacht, and then simplifying it and paring back at night. 'If there is jewellery, there must be a lot. If it's real, that's showy and in bad taste,' she said. 'The jewellery I make is fake and very beautiful. Even more beautiful than the real thing.'

"If there is jewellery, there must be a lot. If it's real, that's showy and in bad taste. The jewellery I make is fake and very beautiful. Even more beautiful than the real thing."

The most iconic Chanel accessory of all is her perfume. She was one of the first designers to introduce her own, beginning with the iconic Chanel N°5 in 1921, as she believed that the essential finishing touch to any gown was scent. She even proclaimed that 'a woman who doesn't wear perfume has no future' and that it should be sprayed 'wherever you expect to be kissed'.

Ernest Beaux, a Russian master perfumer, helped Chanel design her first perfume, creating it in his laboratory in Grasse, in the South of France. She wanted it to be a blend of floral notes and to cling to the skin like a silk gown. This was achieved by the novel use of aldehydes. Beaux gave Chanel a choice of ten scents, and she selected number five, her lucky number; which also made it sound like a scientific sample.

The glass bottle of Chanel N°5 was simple and modern, like that of a man's toiletry bottle, and suited the Art Deco sensibilities of the time. Launched in 1921, the perfume was marketed to be the most exclusive, her sales girls spraying it in her salons to intrigue wealthy customers. Her second perfume, N°22, launched in 1922, followed by Gardénia in 1925, Bois des Iles in 1926 and Cuir de Russie in 1927.

Play with
Past **Successes**

Chanel's longevity as the world's leading designer for seven decades could partly be explained by the consistency in her creations. Chanel devised a series of rules in her designs to create a timeless uniform: easy jersey pieces, a little tweed suit with the cardigan-style jacket and knee-length skirt, the Little Black Dress and the strings of pearls, all of which allowed a woman to feel comfortable, relaxed and beautiful. By the 1960s, Chanel had a well-established formula in place, meeting the expectations of her clients who wished to buy into the Chanel allure. She once said: 'Dress shabbily and they remember the dress; dress impeccably and they remember the woman.'

On 5 February 1954, fashion editors and buyers gathered at 31 Rue Cambon in anticipation of 71-year-old Chanel's first collection in fifteen years. While there was some disappointment that her designs were merely a tribute to a style she had forged in the 1920s, American women were quick to appreciate the smart elegance of her jackets, skirts and simple dresses. *Elle*'s editor Hélène Gordon-Lazareff, envisioned the suit as for 'the modern women, for voting, wage-earning, independent women … with no time to waste'.

The Chanel suit became a uniform and, just like the LBD, it was a style that she came back to time and time again because she knew that it was a formula for success. 'Elegance in a garment is freedom of movement,' she said.

With a Chanel suit, customers across the decades knew exactly what they were getting. Even in the 1960s, when young, hip designers like Yves Saint Laurent, André Courrèges and Paco Rabanne played with

→ A twist on the classic Chanel aesthetic of black dress, quilted handbag, cuff bracelets and glittering logo belt, at Paris Fashion Week in October 2018.

new shapes and textiles, Chanel stayed with
what she knew best, stubbornly keeping the
hemline on the knee. During the swinging
1960s this seemed outdated, but by 1970
Chanel's classic style hit the right note for
those exhausted with hippie and mod styles.

She believed she had a duty to keep on
producing her classic style so that women
could access well-crafted clothing that
brought them freedom and confidence.

Bettina Ballard observed in 1960, 'The
"Chanel look" remains exactly the same
and precisely what women seem to want.
Her extraordinary comeback in 1954 – a
comeback that has endured – had far more
to do with a real hunger that women had for
the confidence-giving clothes that Gabrielle
Chanel had always understood, always made,
than any striking innovation that she brought
to fashion.'

"Dress shabbily and they remember the dress; dress impeccably and they remember the woman."

Chanel

The
Inspiration

Don't Forget your **Past**

The convent at Aubazine Abbey, isolated in the remote chestnut and pine-covered hills of the Auvergne region, is the key to the creative mind of Chanel.

Chanel's father was a peddler and her early years were spent at cheap lodgings in bustling market towns, filled with the sounds of tradespeople. But after her mother died, when Coco was twelve, she was sent to the abbey with her two sisters. The convent there was quiet and contemplative in comparison to the itinerant life with her parents, and it shaped her love for simplicity, cleanliness and order. Her appreciation of black and white can also be traced back to

the monochrome of the Cistercian convent. Black was the colour of the nuns' habits and the dark recesses of the abbey; white was the colour of the bed sheets and petticoats washed in the laundry; beige, the natural stone of the abbey walls.

The rosary-style necklaces, celestial jewels, and Maltese crosses, which featured on her famous 1937 white enamel cuff bracelet, can also be traced back to this time, where these shapes were formed in a stone mosaic in the corridors, along with crescent moons, five-pointed stars and eight-petal flowers. The simple pattern in the colourless windows of the abbey, which followed the austere rules of the Cistercian order, even inspired the double C logo.

Edmonde Charles-Roux, one-time French *Vogue* editor, wrote: 'Whenever she began yearning for austerity, for the ultimate in cleanliness, for faces scrubbed with yellow soap; or waxed nostalgic for all things white, simple and clean, for linen piled high in cupboards, white-washed walls … one had to

→ The classic Coco Chanel aesthetic of black dresses with contrasting white collars, like that of a convent schoolgirl, referenced her childhood spent at Aubazine Abbey. From the Chanel Métiers d'Art fashion show in Rome, December 2015.

"One had to understand she was speaking a secret code, and that every word she uttered meant only one word, Aubazine."

French writer Edmonde Charles-Roux

understand she was speaking a secret code, and that every word she uttered meant only one word, Aubazine.'

It was unlikely that Chanel's wealthy clients understood the reason behind her design choices. Chanel maintained secrecy about her childhood, as she was afraid she would be considered illegitimate because her parents were unmarried when she was born. Instead she improvised, and like a real-life Gatsby, used her charm to gain entry into high society. She re-imagined the nuns as maiden aunts dressed in black, and recounted that it was they who taught her to hem sheets and stitch crosses onto nightgowns. She credited her aunts for her sense of order, 'for having things done right, for chests filled with linens that smell good, and gleaming floors'.

← Inspired by the symbols of Aubazine Abbey, Maltese crosses featured on cuff bracelets and on chain belts in the Chanel autumn-winter 2020–21 show.

Embrace your Social Circle

When Chanel followed Étienne Balsan from Moulins to his countryside estate outside Paris, she found herself in a world of actresses, aristocratic sportsmen and cocottes. Among Balsan's guests at Royallieu was his mistress, Émilienne d'Alençon, a celebrity courtesan and former mistress of King Leopold II of Belgium.

Chanel looked different in her simple jackets and straw boaters, like a convent schoolgirl rather than a kept woman, and after admiring the hats she had created, Émilienne chose to wear a boater to the races. Its simplicity looked different against the fashion for ostentation, and other courtesans immediately wondered where Émilienne had found such a design. Chanel bought a stock of straw boaters

→ Courtesan and stage star Émilienne d'Alençon was one of the first Parisian women to fall for Coco Chanel's designs.

from Galeries Lafayette in Paris to keep up with demand, and added 'just a touch of something on top', with ribbons or hatpins.

Wishing to find her own independence rather than being dependent, like the courtesans, Chanel persuaded Balsan to let her sell her hats from his Paris bachelor pad at 160 boulevard Malesherbes. Among her clients were his actress friends such as Gabrielle Dorziat, who wore Chanel's hats when appearing on stage in *Bel Ami*. In 1913, Chanel made one of her first dresses for actress Suzanne Orlandi – a simple dark velvet dress with a contrasting white collar.

Chanel frequently used the actresses in her circle to help promote her hats and garments. In September 1909, popular stage star Lucienne Roger wore a Chanel hat on the cover of the fashion magazine *Comoedia Illustré*. It was a fantastic piece of publicity that proved so popular that, in the following issue Chanel was invited to model two of her own designs herself. In January 1911, actress Jeanne Dirys appeared on a *Comoedia*

"I had a good deal of luck. I went out with well-known people. Everyone was in raptures."

Chanel

Illustré cover in an illustration by Paul Iribe, who would later be a lover of Chanel's. 'I had a good deal of luck,' Chanel later reflected. 'I went out with well-known people. Everyone was in raptures: "Where did you find that hat? Who made that dress?"'

Parisian society ladies were curious to see this little gamine who had taken the heart of Balsan and Boy Capel; they flocked to her first boutique, Chanel, Modes, when it opened in January 1910 on Rue Cambon.

As her salons became a mecca for the rich and well-connected, Chanel used society ladies like Lady Diana Cooper and

Iya, Lady Abdy, to further publicise her designs. Vera Bate, a friend of the Duke of Westminster, was hired as a model and public relations expert, using her invaluable social connections to the British aristocracy to help promote Chanel's designs. Chanel said she employed society people 'because they were useful to me and because they got around Paris, working on my behalf'.

Her time spent at Royallieu, surrounded by the finely dressed women of the Belle Époque, also served to inspire later designs. In the 1930s, as the world embraced the romantic to escape the reality of the Depression, Chanel thought back to her days at the racetrack with the courtesans. While she had originally rejected the restricted, overly ornate fashions of the time, she paid tribute to it now through long tulle and lace gowns, a modernised version of the pre-war confections.

← Lily-Rose Depp, one of Karl Lagerfeld's modern muses, modelling a spectacular frothy pink wedding gown during the spring-summer 2017 Chanel show at Paris Fashion Week.

Use your
Own Image

Chanel was aware that to find success, she needed more than a name. She had to build a public persona. From her days as a milliner, Chanel used her own chic image and gamine features to sell her hats by modelling them in magazines. 'In the grandstands, people began talking about my amazing, unusual hats,' she recounted. 'I was the curious creature, the little woman whose straw boater fitted her head, and whose head fitted her shoulders.'

She captured the imagination of the well-heeled visitors to Deauville as the mistress of Boy Capel, who was also that rare creature – an independent woman. Such was her celebrity, that she was drawn by celebrity cartoonist Sem in the newspaper *Le Figaro*, with Boy Capel depicted as a polo playing centaur. 'I became something of a celebrity, and ... I started a fashion – couturiers as stars. Before my time that didn't exist.'

When she arrived at her salon in her Rolls Royce, Chanel was the epitome of success. She promoted a lifestyle that attracted the wealthiest women, only too happy to splash their money on buying into the Chanel brand. She used her modernity, her bobbed hair and her slim figure to create a style that captured her own essence – one of freedom.

Before 1914, women were rounder, their bodies cinched into shape with corsetry, but Chanel took credit for launching the new body shape that defined the flapper. 'By inventing the jersey, I liberated the body, I discarded the waist ... I created a new shape; in order to conform to it all my customers, with the help of the war, became slim. Women came to me to buy their slim figures.'

Chanel was the first female designer whose name elicited excitement and whose love affairs hit the headlines, such as the anticipation of an engagement with the Duke of Westminster in the mid-1920s. There were few designers who were mentioned in the society pages alongside their clients. *Vogue*, in 1924, described how Chanel wore 'the designs her clients love with so much chic herself ... that her daring provokes admiration; her success applause!'

↑ At Chanel's autumn-winter 2001–2 show, Pop Art photos of Chanel were branded on striped sweaters, as her image became as coveted as the clothes themselves.

Speak the Language of Revolution

Chanel once said: 'Fashion should express the place, the moment. This is where the commercial adage "the client is always right" get its precise and clear meaning; that meaning demonstrates that fashion, like opportunity, is something that has to be grabbed by the hair.'

Coco Chanel was a couturiere with an inherent knowledge of what her customers needed, even before they did. When she first arrived in Paris, in 1906, she observed the women trussed up in lace, ruffles and elaborate hats. 'I sensed that women were tired of ludicrous trimmings and fussy bits and pieces, and the answer was bone-simple clothes,' she said, adding that she wanted to remove restrictive undergarments, 'because women cannot work while they are imprisoned in a corset'.

→ Consuelo Crespi, Italian countess and fashion editor, demonstrating how the Chanel suit was perfect for independent women in the 1950s.

She experienced this for herself when she wore a tightly corseted blue and white gown to dinner with Boy Capel at the Café de Paris. It was so constraining that she had to undo it after eating and couldn't close the fastenings again. Panicking at humiliating herself in public, she promised to never wear a corset again.

Aristocrats like Lady Kitty de Rothschild, Antoinette Bernstein and Paris's leading actress, Cécile Sorel, were attracted to Chanel's jersey designs during the First World War, as they suited the wartime austerity and demand for practicality, yet were imbued with a sense of luxury. In Paris, Chanel, Modes was in the perfect position close to the Ritz, as the hotel, with its best-heated interior in Paris, was a popular place for ladies to lunch and to meet the Allied officers who gathered there. When they wandered over to her boutique, Chanel would listen into their conversations to find out their needs, such as warmer coats and sports frocks for when the war was over.

"Fashion should express the place, the moment ... fashion, like opportunity, is something that has to be grabbed by the hair."

Chanel

Up until her self-imposed hiatus at the outbreak of the Second World War, Chanel provided clothing that suited the mood of the times – the freedom-giving sportswear and flapper dresses in the 1920s, the feminine gowns that offered an escape from the turmoil of the 1930s and the dependable suits for busy women.

While Chanel's comeback collection, in 1954, was at first met with scepticism by the French fashion press, her reliable designs offered a respite from the elaborate concoctions of Dior's New Look. 'Femininity had gone too far,' said Pat Cunningham, fashion editor of *Vogue*, on the post-war fashions. 'You needed stage-coach luggage to pack your frocks in and ladies' maids to fix the trimmings and petticoats. Chanel simplified clothes to meet modern needs.'

Choose **Love** as an **Influence**

Chanel liked to cast a sartorial eye on her lovers' wardrobes. They were very rich men, polo players and country sport enthusiasts at the centre of high society, and they gifted her with precious stones and ropes of pearls. Yet she found value in borrowing their clothing; tweed jackets to keep warm or a jersey sweater for taking part in sports.

Chanel was first drawn to masculine clothing from her days at Royallieu, where she borrowed Étienne Balsan's shirt and tie to go horse-riding, snipping at them with scissors to cut them to suit her. Feeling a chill while watching Boy Capel play polo at Deauville one day, she pulled on his jersey polo sweater, adding a handkerchief as a belt

→ Chanel's love affair with the Duke of Westminster led to a life-long affiliation with Scotland, as shown in the Scottish tweeds and tartans at the 2012 Métiers d'Art fashion show at Linlithgow Palace.

and rolling up her sleeves. It inspired her to create her own feminine sweaters and turtlenecks.

Chanel's love affairs with Igor Stravinsky and Grand Duke Dmitri Pavlovich served to influence her Russian collection in 1923, with its intricate embroidery and nod to a Russian silhouette, and later, in 1927, the perfume Cuir de Russie. Chanel was fascinated by the aristocratic Russians who came to Paris after the 1917 revolution. She said that 'every Westerner should have succumbed to "Slavic charm" to know what it is. I was captivated.'

Through Boy Capel, Chanel learned the rules of upper-class society and when she took up with Hugh Grosvenor, the Second Duke of Westminster, she threw herself into country pursuits with gusto. She admired the British aristocrats with their tweeds passed down the generations, impeccably pressed shirts and polished shoes which they favoured over fashion fads.

After borrowing the Duke's hunting jackets to wear on his vast Reay Forest

"A woman who cuts her hair is about to change her life."

→ Chanel in 1929, modelling her long tweed cardigans and pleated skirts, heavily influenced by the Duke of Westminster's tweed hunting jackets and which reflected her affinity for the British look.

estate in the Highlands, she was inspired to incorporate the look into her own range. In the late 1920s, she created a softer, cardigan-like version of the tweed jacket and teamed it with pleated skirts and ropes of pearls for her sporty daywear.

When the Duke married another woman, possibly because Chanel was unable to secure him a male heir, the designer claimed she was bored with the excesses of his filthy rich lifestyle. 'God knows I wanted love. But the moment I had to choose between the man I loved and my dresses, I chose the dresses,' Chanel stated.

Express your
Artistic Temperament

From the moment she first moved to Paris, Chanel's life was progressive, independent and sexually liberated. Her avant-garde style ingratiated her into the circle of Cubists, surrealists, modernists and futurists, including Pablo Picasso, Jean Cocteau, Igor Stravinsky, Pierre Reverdy, the group of composers known as Les Six and her closest female friend, Misia Sert.

This circle in Paris not only socialised together at extravagant costume balls and artist hang-outs like the nightclub Le Boeuf sur le Toit, but teamed up to work on avant-garde operas and ballets. In 1922, Jean Cocteau asked Chanel to design the costumes for his stage adaptation of *Antigone*, because Chanel 'is the greatest couturière of our age, and it is impossible to imagine the daughters of Oedipus poorly dressed'. She created costumes for Cocteau's 1924's *Le Train Bleu* and featured a curtain designed by Picasso and choreography by Bronislava Nijinska.

Throughout her life, Chanel was an ambassador for the arts. She was incredibly generous, financially supporting Jean Cocteau and funding Stravinsky and Sergei Diaghilev's works, including the revival of *The Rite of Spring* in 1920. She worked with Jean Renoir to provide costumes for *La Bête Humaine* (1938) and *La Règle du Jeu* (1939), where she dressed the French aristocrat characters in tweed hunting clothes.

Chanel was also very encouraging of film directors like Roger Vadim, François Truffaut and Luchino Visconti, providing costumes for their La Nouvelle Vague films. Coco said: 'Money makes it possible to help people one admires ... I gave the Ballets Russes a great deal of help, and I asked only one thing: that no one know about it.'

→ Chanel's costumes for Salvador Dalí's the *Bacchanale* ballet featured in *Vogue* in 1939. The two artists were good friends, with Dalí painting some of his most important works in the 1930s at La Pausa, Chanel's French Riviera home.

Arouse the **Trailblazers**

In the bohemian Paris of the 1920s, Chanel was admired by the uninhibited women of the city, such as Tara de Lempicka, Princess Violette Murat, Nancy Cunard and Daisy Fellowes, who set the city ablaze with their shocking antics while turned out in beautiful Chanel gowns.

Hollywood actress Louise Brooks epitomised the fresh modernity of Chanel with her bobbed hair, flapper dresses and strings of pearls set against a stark black gown. It was an image completely indebted to Coco. The socialite Boni de Castellane said that 'women no longer exist; all that's left are the boys created by Chanel'.

And just as Chanel inspired the rich, the beautiful and the talented, she looked to them. In the 1920s, Chanel used Hollywood

→ This iconic 1928 image of the Jazz Age star Louise Brooks was symbolic of the Chanel look, with her bobbed hair, black flapper dress and string of pearls.

actresses to model her clothes, as she had the foresight to pick up on their international headline-grabbing appeal. Ina Claire, a former Ziegfeld Follies' chorus girl who was hailed as the next big thing in Hollywood, has been a customer of Chanel's since 1926. Chanel, in turn, hired her to model shimmering gowns and tailored suits to generate publicity in the United States. The actress wore a Chanel black suit trimmed with red fox fur in the 1930 film *The Royal Family of Broadway*.

While Chanel saw the benefits in dressing movie stars, Hollywood, trying to establish itself as the fashion capital of the world, looked to the designer to bring a sense of authority to the costumes on screen. Chanel was lured to Hollywood for a $1 million contract with Samuel Goldwyn Productions in 1931, where she was greeted by the biggest stars of the day, including Marlene Dietrich, Greta Garbo and Katharine Hepburn; three women who were lauded for their unconventional and androgynous style. Chanel was particularly pleased when Garbo

commented that 'without you I wouldn't have made it, with my little hat and my raincoat'.

Chanel designed costumes for three films: the Busby Berkeley-choreographed musical *Palmy Days*; *The Greeks Had a Word for Them*, which starred Ina Claire as one of three gold-digging chorus girls; and *Tonight or Never*, where she dressed Gloria Swanson in a black bias-cut gown. The elegant simplicity of Chanel costumes was not considered sensational enough for the screen, and Chanel quickly grew tired of the movie colony. Yet Hollywood stars would continue to be spellbound by her designs and after her comeback, in 1954, she attracted the biggest stars in the world to her salon, such as Lauren Bacall, Grace Kelly and Elizabeth Taylor.

"Women no longer exist; all that's left are the boys created by Chanel."

Boni de Castellane

↖ Joan Blondell, Ina Claire and Madge Evans in *The Greeks Had a Word for Them* (1932). The beach pyjamas Chanel designed for Ina Claire set a trend after being hailed by *Vogue*.

← Gloria Swanson visited Chanel's Rue Cambon salon for her costume fittings for *Tonight or Never* (1931). While she created timeless designs, such as this black dress, the costumes were deemed too unshowy for Hollywood's tastes.

Harness
the **Dramatic**

Chanel was a romantic at heart, and her love of drama and the arts heavily influenced her designs. 'It was a lucky thing for me that I had read all those books, because I came to Paris at a very romantic time, the time of the Ballets Russes,' Chanel once said. 'It was when I saw the Diaghilev ballet that I decided I was going to live in what I loved.'

Sergei Diaghilev's Ballets Russes created a sensation when it burst into Paris theatres in 1909. The energetic, modernist choreography and the colourful costumes, which took the audience to faraway places, made a huge impact on the tastes of Parisian society. Chanel was intoxicated by its exotic spectacle, and it shaped her love of Eastern arts and intricate details, such as folklore-

→ *Vogue* in September 1939, featured this striking image of Chanel watching over one of her models in a silk velvet suit, from her 'Watteau collection'. It was a dramatic finale as she closed her business on the outbreak of the Second World War.

inspired embroidery. She decorated her Parisian apartments with eighteenth-century red and black lacquered coromandel screens, painted with the Eastern iconography of kimonoed women, birds, fish and flowers.

Following the revolution of 1917, a number of Russian aristocrats and artists fled to Paris with their folk traditions and arts. Chanel was drawn to Russian émigrés like Stravinsky and Diaghilev; she employed some of them in her business and incorporated Slavic elements into her dramatic Russian collection of 1923, considered her most important since her Biarritz collection of 1916. These included a belted roubachka blouse, a striped telnyashka undershirt and folklore embroidery on velvet or crepe de Chine blouses.

Chanel looked to the history books when she created her first jewellery collection. With its Byzantine and Renaissance influences, it was heavy on drama and conjured up portraits of Elizabeth I, with her multiple ropes of pearls, and Mary Queen of

← Chanel's autumn-winter collection in 1993 displayed Byzantine-inspired dramatic couture, shimmering with gold and silver appliqué, like that of her Russian collection in 1923.

Scots, with her heavy crucifixes on chains. Chanel's jewelled crosses and lustrous pearls offered a striking contrast against the black mousseline or crepe de Chine of her gowns.

Fashions in the 1930s embraced a dramatic feminine silhouette, and Chanel amplified this by inserting shoulder pads into jackets to enhance the waist. In 1938, she created a black velvet 'Watteau' suit, which took inspiration from the eighteenth-century paintings of Jean-Antoine Watteau, contrasting it with the white ruffles of a blouse. As a final dramatic flourish before the outbreak of war in 1939, Chanel embraced the red, white and blue of the French flag in a number of patriotic pieces.

"The best colour in the whole world is the one that looks good on you."

Look to your **Location**

While Chanel's creations represented the modernity and excitement of Paris, she was also inspired by the places she visited.

Chanel opened her boutique in Deauville in 1913, at a time when it was the fashionable summer beach resort for Parisian society, who flocked to its racetrack and casino, and enjoyed the bracing sea air of the Normandy coastline. 'I was in the right place, an opportunity beckoned. I took it,' she said. 'What was needed was simplicity, comfort, neatness: unwittingly I offered all of that.'

Chanel looked at the way society people flaunted their style on the promenade, and then added her own revolutionary twist, with practical, easy-to-wear turtlenecks, linen skirts and sailor blouses. Observing the sailors and fishermen in their striped

sweaters, she made a luxury female version that could be slipped on over the head.

After meeting the Duke of Westminster at the end of 1923, Chanel was introduced to the style of the British aristocracy, after which she consistently used tweed for her jackets. When she opened her London fashion house in the heart of Mayfair in 1927, she created a range of fashions to fit with the calendar of British high society – gowns for debutantes during the coming out season, afternoon dresses for Ascot and sportswear for visiting a country estate.

Chanel was a frequent guest on board the Duke of Westminster's yacht, the *Flying Cloud*, and the navy blue and white uniforms worn by the crew inspired a range of designs. Her white skirts and tops featured navy stripes, and she created her own version of the yachting caps. In 1926, *Vogue* carried a fashion spread on board a yacht, which featured Chanel's natural jersey sports dresses with pleated skirts and cardigans with nautical stripes. 'Navy

→ The Venice Lido inspired Chanel's resort style of white beach pyjamas and striped tops, and was a backdrop for the Chanel Cruise 2010 fashion show.

"I was in the right place, an opportunity beckoned. I took it ..."

Chanel

and white are the only possible colours. The Navy's colours,' Chanel once said.

Venice was another place that shaped Chanel's aesthetic. She first visited the city with Misia and José Sert in 1920 to recover from the death of Boy Capel, and found comfort in the Byzantine churches and museums. She was struck by the beauty of the city; the gold of St Mark's Basilica, the vivid colours in the paintings of Caravaggio and Tintoretto, the glamour of the Lido and the Venice lion, which became her own personal talisman.

While Rue Cambon is the spiritual home of Chanel, where she kept a salon from 1910, she chose to permanently live at the Hôtel Ritz until her death in 1971. As she gazed out of the windows of the hotel onto Place Vendôme, its octagonal shape may have inspired her design for the simple Chanel Nº5 bottle.

Feel the Heat

All her life Chanel worshipped the sun.
She was pictured on the beach at Saint Jean-de-Luz in 1915, with Boy Capel, wearing a dark bathing suit, which was considered incredibly risqué at a time when women were expected to cover up on the beach and shield their skin with parasols. Suntans were a marker of the poor, as it signified working outdoors, but for Chanel it meant good health and the luxury of time. She remarked after observing pale American girls on the beach at the Venice Lido: 'How much more beautiful these young women would be ... how brightly their jewellery would glitter if worn on a skin bronzed by the sun.'

Chanel wasn't the first to come to the Riviera at the height of summer, when it was only fashionable to visit during the cooler winter months. She was inspired by American bohemians like Sara and Gerald Murphy and F. Scott and Zelda Fitzgerald, who spent summers in Antibes in the early 1920s. Chanel first went to the South of France to try to heal after Capel's death, seeking refuge in the scent of flowers carried on the warm Côte d'Azur air, and it inspired her first perfume, N°5, with its notes of jasmine, ylang-ylang, neroli and May rose.

Chanel further captured the essence of the Riviera when she opened a boutique in Cannes in 1923, selling her range of sports and beachwear. As well as the tan, Chanel popularised white beach pyjamas, after she was photographed wearing her designs at the Venice Lido in 1931. That same year the *New York Times* reported that 'pajamas seem firmly entrenched in fashionable circles ... last summer already saw them dining out in the Casinos of Biarritz and Lido and this

→ Coco Chanel with Duke Laurino of Rome at the Venice Lido in 1937, wearing the white slacks and cork-heeled sandals she popularised.

> # "How much more beautiful these young women would be ... how brightly their jewellery would glitter if worn on a skin bronzed by the sun."
>
> **Chanel**

summer they are taken for granted in the smart resort wardrobe'.

The gardens of Chanel's luxurious Riviera retreat, La Pausa, built in 1929, offered further inspiration for her designs. The purple hues of the lavender in her garden influenced a collection of chiffon dresses and violet velvet suits, and the shimmering blue azure of the Mediterranean were reflected in a number of deep blue gowns.

Her invention of cork-soled sandals was, she reported, sparked by a moment on the Venice Lido. 'I was growing tired of walking barefoot in the hot sand, and because my

leather sandals were burning the soles of my feet, I had a shoemaker on the Zattere cut out a piece of cork in the shape of a shoe and fit two straps to it. Ten years later, the windows of Abercrombie in New York were full of shoes with cork soles.'

→ Chanel was inspired by the azure blue of the Mediterranean Sea, reflective of this shimmering velvet gown worn by Linda Evangelista at the autumn-winter 1990—91 fashion show in Paris.

Appeal to the
Hot New Thing

Just as Coco Chanel was the perfect model for her own clothes, the Chanel woman embodied the same spirit as the designer herself – independence, casual elegance and free-spirited beauty. When she selected her muses, Chanel was drawn to women who were subversive, who wore her clothes with the same flair, and who adopted the same relaxed stance.

Alongside French model Marie-Hélène Arnaud, she also chose flame-haired supermodel Suzy Parker, a Chanel devotee, to front her comeback collection in 1954.

→ French actress Jeanne Moreau, a frequent guest at Rue Cambon, was photographed on the famous mirrored staircase in 1958 wearing the costumes Chanel designed for her for Louis Malle's *The Lovers*.

Chanel recognised the power in using actresses and celebrities as the models for her designs, and Suzy Parker, the all-American girl from Texas, was sure to attract international attention. Parker wore the reincarnated Chanel navy suit with ease as she zipped in and out of cars in Paris, helping to place Chanel as the chic designer for the busy modern woman. Later, Catherine Deneuve would be chosen as the face of Chanel, as she was beautiful, mysterious and had international appeal.

As part of Chanel's support for avant-garde filmmakers, she provided costumes for many New Wave films, and Chanel's muses would include the hot young things of European filmmaking. They could regularly be found in the salon at Rue Cambon. Chanel hailed actress Romy Schneider as her 'ideal woman' and the two became close friends, as they spent time together for lengthy costume fittings for her role in *Boccaccio '70* in 1962, directed by Luchino Visconti.

"They asked ... "What do you wear in bed?" ... So I said, "Chanel Nº5." Because it's the truth!"

Marilyn Monroe

Jeanne Moreau, the darling of New Wave cinema, was another frequent guest at Rue Cambon, discussing literature with Chanel and browsing her bookshelves filled with leather-bound antique works and first editions by friends like Pierre Reverdy. Moreau first modelled for Chanel in 1958, when she posed on the famous staircase in her costumes for Louis Malle's *The Lovers*, her fractured image, repeated in the mirrors on the staircase, coming from every angle.

← Marilyn Monroe would be forever linked with the scent after delivering her famous statement that all she wore in bed was Chanel No5. A series of images of Monroe in New York City in 1955 also documented her ritual of getting ready to go to the theatre, where she held the bottle in her hand as she applied the scent.

French actress Delphine Seyrig wore Chanel for her costumes in the film *Last Year at Marienbad* in 1961, and in François Truffaut's *Stolen Kisses*, where the Rue Cambon boutique served as a backdrop as Seyrig selects a pair of beige and black slingbacks.

While Chanel sought out the women who she believed embodied the Chanel look, the most famous women in the world were also drawn to her. Grace Kelly, Lauren Bacall, Jackie Kennedy and Elizabeth Taylor rocked the classic Chanel jacket and liberally applied Chanel Nº5. As they touched down in Rome, Paris or London, It Girls like Brigitte Bardot, Catherine Deneuve and Jane Fonda faced the whir of photographers in a comfortable Chanel suit, or with the essential accessory, the 2.55 bag, on their arm.

Rebel Against
your Rivals

When Chanel first arrived in Paris, the
fashion scene was dominated by the powerful
couturier Paul Poiret. He shaped the way
society women dressed with his ground-
breaking hobble skirt and lampshade tunics,
and his fluid silhouette which freed women's
bodies from the trappings of the corset.
Poiret was heavily influenced by Asian and
Persian designs, featuring the rich colours of
Arabian Nights, scandalous Turkish-inspired
harem pants and coats shaped like kimonos.

Chanel also sought freedom but she
chose a lighter touch with flexible textiles
like jersey or crepe de Chine. She considered

Poiret to be too fixated on the past and,
when he failed to adapt to the modernity
of the 1920s, Chanel swept in and took his
place as Paris's top designer. Her Little
Black Dress was a rejection of the jewel-
coloured gowns of Poiret. 'For whom are you
mourning?' he was said to have asked her.
'For you, Monsieur,' was her reply.

After the Second World War, Christian
Dior would shape the post-war period with
his 'New Look'. Instead of the utility look
of the war years, he made a striking return
to femininity with corsets, flared skirts and
structured bosoms. Chanel, who had been
in retirement since 1939, was horrified that
fashion was undoing all the freedoms she had
sought to give women. It was the trigger for
Chanel to make her comeback in 1954.

'Men make dresses in which one can't
move,' she once said. 'They tell you very
calmly that the dresses aren't made for
action. I'm frightened when I hear such
things. What will happen when no one else
thinks as I do anymore?'

→ A *Paris Match* editorial in
August 1969 demonstrating the
different skirt length trends, from
the long skirts of Saint Laurent,
to the mid-length of Cardin, Dior,
Bohan and Chanel, and the miniskirts
of Ungaro and Courrèges.

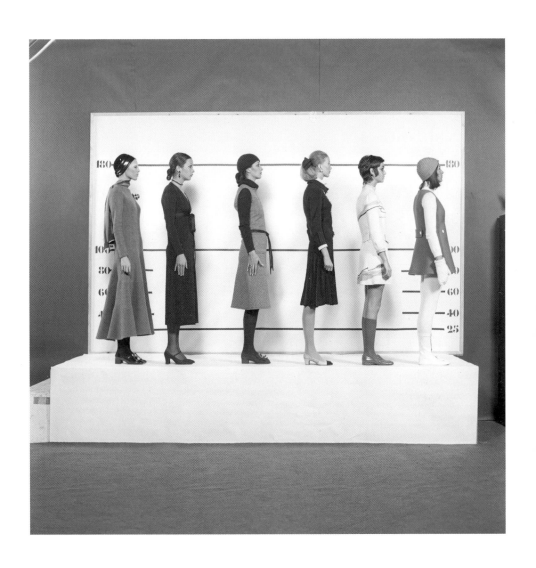

The
Details

Twist Textile **Traditions**

Chanel once proclaimed that 'I built my fortune on an old jersey.' The first pieces of clothing that Chanel sold from her Deauville boutique were jersey sweaters worn with belts, which were inspired by Boy Capel's polo shirts. Jersey was traditionally used for men's underwear and sports clothing, but Chanel found it to be a cost-effective stand-in for scarcer fabrics during the war.

She described how 'there was a shortage of material. I cut jersey from the sweaters the stable lads wore and from the knitted training garments that I wore myself. By the end of the first summer of the war, I had earned two hundred thousand gold francs.'

→ This fluoro-printed jersey polo dress from the spring-summer 2021 collected played on the influence of Boy Capel's jersey polo shirts in Coco Chanel's early collections.

Jersey fabric was supple, easy to wear and readily available, and she credited these jerseys as the origin of the House of Chanel. The fluidity of the fabric meant it could be difficult to cut and manipulate into close-fitting garments, but it suited the style that Chanel was forging. 'Jersey is the hardest fabric to work with, it's a poor fabric; Lord, do I know it! I started out with it,' she said.

In 1916, she bought a surplus quantity of jersey fabric from textile manufacturer Jean Rodier. The jersey was a natural cream colour and she collaborated with Rodier to dye it grey, navy blue, burgundy and pink for her dresses. For her 1916 Biarritz collection, she transformed soft jersey into luxurious couture with striped sweaters, ankle-length skirts, embroidered belted jackets and v-necked chemises, in a rainbow of hues and, by 1917, she was named 'dictator of jersey'. When she opened her Biarritz boutique in 1915, Chanel immediately appealed to the Spanish aristocrats and royalty who were looking for colourful clothing to reflect

→ Model Elizabeth Shevlin in *Vogue*, 1928, wearing Chanel's signature low-waisted jersey dress, with a geometric-printed scarf, and a cloche hat by Agnes.

↘ Chanel reflected in her mirrored staircase at the Rue Cambon salon in 1953, modelling a fluid jersey jacket and skirt, which would define her 1954 comeback.

reflect Spain's neutrality in the war. They snapped up her bright jersey pieces and cotton tunics with large bows at the hips.

In February 1916, *Women's Wear Daily* noted that, 'It is not unusual for smart women to place orders for three or four [Chanel] jersey costumes in different colours at one time.' In the summer of that year, *Vogue* described how jersey 'developed into a passion – a veritable craze'.

Once the war was over, Chanel continued to use jersey for her loose dresses, pleated skirts and striped cardigan jackets. In the 1950s, these jackets were re-imagined for a new generation of active women who felt both comfortable and beautiful in fluid fabric.

"I built my fortune on an old jersey."

Chanel

Choose a Fabric
with **Durability**

Aside from jersey, tweed is the fabric that has come to define Chanel, as its rich texture has shaped the look of her classic jacket since the 1920s. Tweed is a fabric that is timeless, durable and functional. It was a natural fit for the designer who placed great importance on simplicity and practicality. Chanel transformed rough tweed into a soft and feminine fabric, taking it from the countryside to bourgeois city style.

It was on the Duke of Westminster's vast estate in the Scottish Highlands that Chanel fell in love with the ruggedness of the landscape, which matched the textures and colours of the Duke's tweed hunting jackets. Chanel was so inspired by the wildness of the landscape as she fished for salmon, that in 1926 she teamed up with Carlisle

→ A detail of the bouclé tweed from the sky blue Chanel jacket worn by Diana, Princess of Wales in 1997.

tweedmaker William Linton, commissioning soft tweeds in a range of colours, from natural to pastel and jewel tones.

As Chanel inserted the influence of Scotland into her designs, *Vogue*, in 1926, described how: 'Tweed is an essential of the smart new wardrobe.' It showcased a number of her tweed designs, including a dress, a long coat and a suit in green and beige checks which were ideal for playing sports or moving around the city. With her soft tweed cardigans worn with ropes of pearls and a pleated skirt, it was Parisian style with a British twist. The first Chanel tweed jackets were thigh-length and softly tailored. As the 1930s progressed, they became shorter and more structured. Marking her comeback in 1954, the classic bouclé jacket took shape, and it immediately became the much sought-after piece for the independent woman.

Chanel could tell by touch whether a tweed had been made in the Scottish Borders, or if it was a lightweight Italian tweed, and she selected each fabric

depending on which effect she was trying to achieve. For a more structured suit in the 1960s, Chanel chose a heavy wool bouclé and tweeds from designers like Malhia and Bucol. During that period she also began commissioning soft bouclé tweed from Scottish textile designer Bernat Klein to make suits and dresses in colours inspired by the natural world.

Chanel became one of the most prestigious couturieres to champion the textile, and even after her death, the fashion house continued to source from Linton Tweeds in Carlisle to make the classic silk-lined tweed jacket.

↑ Chanel sewing the shoulder of a tweed coat in her Paris workrooms in 1962.

"A woman who doesn't wear perfume has no future."

Find **Magic** in **Numbers**

Five was the number that made Chanel's fortune. It brought her luck, and she used it as a rule in other aspects of her life. Chanel believed in the power of numerology. Her star sign, Leo, was the fifth sign and five was the quintessential number of the cosmos – the *quinta essentia*, or fifth element, added by Aristotle as the essence of the celestial world.

The number was evident in all aspects of Chanel's life. Her collections were held on the fifth of the month, her most famous perfume was named N°5 and her iconic bag was named 2.55, for the month and year it was launched. Ernest Beaux, the perfumer behind Chanel N°5, recalled that she selected the sample labelled number five, because: 'I present my dress collection on the 5th of May … we shall thus leave the number with which it is labelled and this

→ A statement necklace, where the number 5 is brandished like a lucky charm, as part of spring-summer 2015 collection.

number 5 shall bring it good luck.'

Her connection to the number five was so well-known that in 1926 the *New York Times*, reported, 'Chanel always plays the number 5' at the Monte Carlo casino. The myth around the number, inspired by the geometry of Aubazine Abbey, added to the romance and intrigue of her best-selling perfume.

Number 22 also had importance to Chanel, as both she and Boy Capel liked the number 2. He was tragically killed in a car crash at 2 a.m. on 22 December 1919, and in 1922 she launched her N°22 perfume, with its name derived from both the year of its launch and the connection to Boy.

Chanel saw symbolism in the doubling up of objects, like the double C of her name. In her apartment at Rue Cambon she displayed objects in pairs, including two camels on a side table and two life-size deer by her mantelpiece. Perhaps this duality was the pairing of Chanel and Capel, the love of her life and the man who first supported her business.

Embellish with Embroidery

From her first Biarritz collection in 1916, Chanel used embroidery to add intricacy to her simple jersey designs, such as the colourful belted jackets which were teamed with ankle-length skirts. Her embroidery was partly inspired by the romance of the Diaghilev's Ballets Russes, which she had fallen in love with after seeing them for the first time before the war.

Just like the fine details of her beloved coromandel screens that decorated her apartments in Paris, Chanel's embroidery designs frequently looked to Asia. *Vogue*, in 1917, wrote that she was 'making black silk jersey frocks trimmed with Japanese embroidery'. These included white cherry blossoms and gold irises, contrasting beautifully with the dark fabric. A 1918 fur-trimmed black satin evening coat used golden embroidery to create a Turkman-inspired pattern repeated down the front and back.

While she commonly played with jersey for daywear, her satin, velvet and crepe de Chine evening gowns were embroidered with beautiful patterns. Sir Francis Rose described in a *Vogue* essay a Chanel sheath dress of 'black crepe de Chine with shoulder straps was covered with an embroidery of tiny stars and star-like flowers made in almost invisible sequins and diamante beads'.

In 1921, *Vogue* commented that 'the couturiers are still embroidering their way to success', and Chanel continued to be a keen advocate of this technique. She commissioned Dmitri Pavlovich's older

→ The wheat embroidery on this sheer jacket, as part of the Chanel Métiers d'Art 2019–20 show at Le Grand Palais, not only reflected Chanel's love of embroidery, but of how she embraced wheat as a symbol of prosperity.

"The couturiers are still embroidering their way to success."

Vogue

sister, Grand Duchess Maria Pavlovna, to make embroidered fabric through her new business Kitmir. She'd been looking for someone to embroider a Faroe Islands sweater pattern onto silk blouses, and Marie, living a poor existence in exile, offered to provide it at a good price after overhearing Chanel arguing with a seamstress. Using patterns and designs inspired by Slavic folk art, Chanel's Russian collection of 1922 was one of the most important of her career to date. It showcased these embroideries on a black Russian-inspired blouse with wide sleeves, and on a blue georgette crepe day dress, with embroidery creating the shape of a chunky Romanov necklace that was drawn from Maria Pavlovna's memory.

← Chanel's appreciation of skillful embroidery was championed in some of her earliest collections. This was reflected in the intricate detail around the neckline of this dress, as part of the Métiers d'Art fashion show at Linlithgow Palace in 2012. It highlighted the craftsmanship of the fashion house's ateliers in both France and Scotland.

Say it with Stripes

Chanel frequently wore a striped jersey top with navy sailor trousers when in the South of France, adopting a look that suited the climate and making it acceptable for women to embrace such casual androgyny when on holiday.

It was fashionable for bohemians on the Riviera to wear a striped top in the 1920s, with Pablo Picasso and Gerald Murphy throwing on Breton sweaters when on the beach or working in the studio. In the 1950s and 1960s, gamine stars like Audrey Hepburn and Jean Seberg further evoked the spirit of Chanel in striped tops, while Brigitte Bardot's St Tropez-style mixed stripes with Capri pants.

→ Striped sweaters have long been a part of Chanel's summerwear, reminiscent of the jerseys she first sold from her Deauville boutique, like this one from the Chanel Cruise 2020 collection.

Chanel was an early champion of stripes, featuring them in her collections in 1915. In July of that year, *Women's Wear Daily* praised her 'extremely interesting sweaters' made from jersey, which were available in her Deauville boutique. The article continued: 'Striped jersey … in black and white or navy and white, is also employed. These sweaters … slip on the head, opening at the neck for about six inches and are finished with jersey-covered buttons … A great success is predicted for these sweaters.'

Chanel's striped jersey tops referenced the working-class outfits of fishermen and French sailors, whom she had observed during her time on the Normandy coast. The '*marinière*' was first introduced to the uniform of French navy seamen in 1858, with the stripes said to make it easier to spot those who fell overboard.

Chanel continued to incorporate stripes into her sportswear collection as part of her 1920s '*garçonne* look'. A black and white striped sports shirt in jersey, part of the

"Striped jersey ... A great success is predicted for these sweaters."

Women's Wear Daily

collection at the Metropolitan Museum, New York was designed on the bias to create diagonal stripes, and featured a tie at the neck like that of a sailor's blouse.

Chanel was further inspired by the uniforms onboard the Duke of Westminster's yacht, the *Flying Cloud,* for a nautical collection in 1926. Pieces included a beige and blue striped jersey cardigan worn with a blouse and pleated skirt. In 1933, an advertisement in the *Tatler* magazine featured Chanel's long-sleeved hand-knitted striped pullovers with sailor ties at the neck, which came in a variety of colour combinations, and reflected a mix of influences — the navy collar, Riviera stripes and Scottish hand-knits.

← Coco Chanel in the lavender gardens of La Pausa, in 1930. She preferred to wear her easy and relaxed striped jersey tops and wide-legged trousers when staying at her French Riviera retreat.

See it in the Stars

'I love everything that's up high,' Coco Chanel once said. 'The sky, the moon, and I believe in the stars. I was born under the sign of the Lion, like Nostradamus.'

Chanel's fascination with symbolism reached to the sky, and as she was inspired by celestial imagery in her designs it only added to the myth and romance around her life. Through Boy Capel she was introduced to theosophy, a philosophy based on cosmology and the meanings found within the solar system. She was a follower of the zodiac, adopting the lion symbol from her star sign of Leo, and she believed in the magic of numbers, with five having particular significance as the element of the cosmos.

→ Chanel relaxing in her bedroom at La Pausa, where she decorated the bedframe with five-pointed stars, to bring good luck.

In the convent at Aubazine, centuries before Chanel arrived in 1895, the medieval monks used tiny pebbles to create a detailed mosaic on the corridors. These depicted five-pointed stars, a crescent moon and a Maltese cross, and were a reflection of the night sky above the abbey. This imagery may have stayed in the mind of a young girl who trailed up and down the corridors every day.

Chanel referenced these symbols in her homes. She hung five-pointed stars above her bed at La Pausa, her luxury villa on the French Riviera, and in her Rue Cambon apartment she treasured a rare meteorite that crashed to earth in China.

Chanel looked to the stars to create her first diamond collection in 1932, called *Bijoux de Diamants*. While she had championed faux jewellery, this real diamond collection suited the need for glamorous escapism during the Depression. To display them to the public, she decorated wax mannequins with celestial earrings, a comet-like necklace, and a sun-ray tiara, all of which were flexible and adaptable

"In order to
be irreplaceable,
one must always
be different."

in how they could be worn. As Janet Flanner of the *New Yorker* described: 'Chanel's mountings for the jewels are in design dominantly and delicately astronomical. Magnificent lopsided stars for earrings; as a necklace, a superb comet whose nape-encircling tail is all that attaches it to a lady's throat; bracelets that are flexible rays; crescents for hats and hair ...'

Chanel's jewellery continued to be inspired by the celestial, with stars and moons appearing as symbols on brooches, earrings and necklaces, and with stars embroidered on dresses and blouses.

Expose New Parts of the **Body**

When she first sought to free women from the confines of their restrictive dress, Chanel loosened the silhouette around the waist, allowing them to breathe without being held in tightly by a bone corset. She raised the hem to reveal the ankles, making it easier for women to step into a motorcar and to move around the city.

The *garçonne* look of the 1950s exposed the arms and the legs, allowing women to dance freely to the Charleston. Over the decade, hem lengths shifted, but Chanel chose to keep it just below the knee. She was consistent in her mission to dress the active, modern woman in pursuit of freedom. 'I now had customers who were busy women,' she said. 'A busy woman needs to feel

→ While most attention fell on the iconic suit jacket following Chanel's comeback in 1954, her beautifully romantic lace dresses were a key element of her collection in the 1950s.

comfortable in her clothes. You need to be able to roll up your sleeves.'

Skirt lengths dropped following the Depression, and the shape of a woman's body emerged as bias-cut gowns clung to curves. Chanel shifted the erogenous zone from the legs to the back, creating beautiful gowns that plunged behind, revealing bare skin that was lightly touched with a string of pearls. Chanel also exposed the shoulders, adding a sensuality to that part of the body with her strapless gowns. *Vogue,* in July 1938, praised her romantic black lace dress with bare shoulders. 'At a time when evening dresses were strapped or v-necked, she had completely bared the shoulders and freed the figure, starting a whole new evening trend,' wrote *Vogue* editor Bettina Ballard.

As designers like Christian Dior showcased their cinched, structured gowns in the 1950s, Chanel returned to a simple silhouette with a range of strapless black or white lace cocktail dresses that placed the focus on the bare skin around the shoulders

"At a time when evening dresses were strapped or v-necked, she had completely bared the shoulders and freed the figure, starting a whole new evening trend."

Vogue editor Bettina Ballard

and neckline. Chanel developed her own instincts around what parts of the female body to expose and to cover and she refused to shift her method purely for fashion fads.

'The art of couture lies in knowing how to enhance,' she once said. 'Raising the waist in front to make the woman appear taller; lowering the back to avoid sagging bottoms. The dress must be cut longer at the back because it rides up. Everything that makes the neck longer is attractive.'

↑ Model Stella Tennant made waves in this microscopic bikini at Chanel's spring-summer 1996 show.

← The belly button was the erogenous zone in the 1990s, and Karl Lagerfeld in 1995 tweaked the classic suit for a bohemian stomach reveal.

Faux Jewellery
can be **Priceless**

Chanel liked to break the rules of how to wear jewellery. She piled on the strings of pearls and heavy necklaces during the day, pared it back in the evening. By championing the fake over the precious, she further democratised fashion.

Chanel commissioned jeweller Augustine Gripoix to create her first jewel collection in 1924. Instead of real gems, they used acrylic, plexiglass and pâte de verre, a technique that melted glass into gold frames. While Chanel championed fake jewellery, she was inspired by the rubies and emeralds she was given by the Duke of Westminster, and long gilt chains with pearls and jewel-encrusted crosses from Dmitri Pavlovich. Inspired by her surroundings, she would relax on her beige suede sofa at Rue Cambon, playing with a mix of stones to spark ideas.

→   The ropes of faux pearls which Coco Chanel first introduced in the 1920s have continued to be a feature in every Chanel collection.

This first collection was indebted to the Byzantine and Renaissance periods, with ropes of faux pearls and pâte de verre Maltese crosses. Strings of pearls became an essential for every Parisian woman. *Vogue* championed Chanel's large iridescent pearls, reminding readers they were better than the real thing. The long ropes complemented the silhouette and dripped down the front of a black silk gown or an exposed back. One of her most famous pieces, created in collaboration with Duke Fulco Di Verdura in 1937, was a wide white enamel bracelet set with multi-coloured stones in a Maltese cross. These embellished cuffs would remain an important element of her jewellery collections.

Chanel professed not to like ostentatious jewellery and chose to create clip-on earrings, necklaces and decorative brooches over heavy-set precious gems. She wore her own imitation jewellery alongside expensive jewels, and by leading the way, knew that her wealthy clients would follow.

Don't Shy
from the **Glitz**

While Chanel built a fashion empire on the simplicity of her silhouette, forging a reputation as the modernist designer, her gowns were incredibly detailed in their embellishments. Her use of sequins, fringing and beading showcased complex workmanship, were unashamedly romantic and further lifted her couture into the extraordinary. 'Adornment, what a science! Beauty, what a weapon! Modesty, what elegance,' she once proclaimed.

Chanel's intricate flapper dresses in the 1920s were perfect for dancing the Charleston, as they offered freedom of movement and shimmered under the lights. Silk georgette and silk velvet were decorated with silver beaded fringing and rhinestone, and flexible knits were infused with sequins, evoking the Chinese lacquered screens that

she displayed in her homes. *Vogue*, in 1924, featured model Alden Gay in a black and white georgette crepe gown covered with a cascade of jet and crystal beads, while another evening gown that year featured heavy gold lace embroidered with beads. These dresses fitted with the Art Deco aesthetic that would become de rigueur following the 1925 International Exhibition of Modern Decorative and Industrial Arts in Paris.

Lace was another favourite material of Chanel's, initially decorating her First World War jersey frock coats with intricate panels and sleeve trimmings. Fussy lace did not quite fit with the streamlined aesthetic of the Jazz Age, but at the beginning of the 1930s, as the Great Depression called for an escape to the past and a return to the feminine, Chanel revisited the Belle Époque with tiers of lace and organdie frills.

Chanel's 1937 collection was all about the drama, featuring extravagant evening wear decorated with heavy sequins. A striking

→ The shimmering sequins in the form of tiny camellias add to the romance of this floor-length gown from Chanel's haute couture autumn-winter 2019–20 show.

"Adornment, what a science! Beauty, what a weapon! Modesty, what elegance."

Chanel

trouser suit with bolero jacket was covered entirely in rows of sequins, contrasting with its light lace and chiffon blouse, and was worn by *Harper's Bazaar* editor Diana Vreeland, who always strove to make an impact with what she wore. This style would later be revitalised in the 1960s, as Chanel created a range of embroidered silk and glitter tweed trouser suits.

Perhaps one of the most symbolic of her sequin designs was an evening gown worn by Countess Madeleine de Montgomery to Lady Mendl's seventy-fifth birthday party in 1939. With its colourful sequin decoration in the shape of fireworks, it dramatically marked the end of the decade and the start of the Second World War. By using such detailed decoration to add a touch of the exotic to a simple silhouette, Chanel was very much ahead her time.

Discover your Own Motif

As her favourite flower, the simple white camellia appeared in many different guises in the designs of Chanel. The image of the camellia flower was formed in the stitches of embroidery on a blouse, as a print on fabric, or fashioned as an embellishment in silk, chiffon, organza or tweed. And because it was scentless, the real flower could be pinned as a corsage on a black dress, where it would not compete with perfume.

The camellia was traditionally associated with the Parisian demimonde, when it was worn to symbolise the courtesan who was available to be seduced, and was represented by the doomed character of Marguerite Gautier in Alexandre Dumas' novel, *La Dame aux Camélias*. Chanel recollected how enthralled she was as a thirteen-year-old when she saw Sarah

Bernhardt star in the Art Nouveau stage version at the Renaissance Theatre in Paris in 1896. The tragic romance stirred within Chanel a memory of her mother dying from consumption, and inspired her future love of camellias. '*La Dame aux Camélias* was my life, all the trashy novels I'd fed on,' she said.

Once Chanel emerged from the world of kept women at Royallieu, finding her own freedom through work, she held onto the symbol of the camellia. It came to represent the death of a courtesan. Moreover, the flower was appealing for its scent, much like the freshness of the one worn by Émiliene d'Alençon. Gentlemen in the Belle Époque also pinned the flower to the buttonholes of their jackets and tunics as a sign of refinement, and she took this sign and used it for her androgynous designs.

In a photo on the beach at Étretat in 1913, Chanel modelled her own jersey jacket and skirt, and pinned a camellia flower into the loose fabric belt. From 1923 she began stitching white corsages onto dark

↑ Delicate camellias were
embroidered onto the sheer bodice
of an evening gown, for Chanel's
haute couture spring-summer
2020 fashion show in Paris.

→ Resembling the shape of a
camellia flower, this dress was
part of Chanel's ready-to-wear
spring-summer 2012 collection.

"La Dame aux Camélias was my life, all the trashy novels I'd fed on."

Chanel

chiffon gowns, where they stood out as brilliant illuminations against the inky black. *Vogue*, in 1926, featured actress Ina Claire modeling a sleeveless evening dress which was embroidered in silver beads and metal, forming an intricate pattern of camellias.

As well as embossing the camellia onto the gilt buttons of her tweed jackets, the symbol was a consistent favourite in Chanel's jewellery collections. If you look carefully, you can find the camellia pattern traced delicately in embroidery and on beading on gowns, pinned to jackets, decorating dresses and within Chanel's apartments; in a vase of rock-crystal camellias, painted onto coromandel screens and as an emblem in her smoked crystal chandelier.

Find your
Spirit Animal

Chanel was born under the star sign of Leo, on 19 August 1883, and she used its lion symbol in many aspects of her life. The lion symbolised power and commanded attention, and it meant so much to her that five lions were carved into the headstone of her grave at Lausanne cemetery in Switzerland.

Just as the other symbols of Chanel's life stemmed from Aubazine, there were carved lion-like creatures within the abbey. Her early childhood was one where she had to fight for survival, and she said that like the lion, 'I use my claws to prevent people from doing me harm, but, believe me, I suffer more from scratching than from being scratched.'

Chanel called Boy Capel the 'lion of London society' whom she had tamed. After he was killed in a car crash in December 1919, one of her trips to aid her recovery was to

Venice. The symbol of Venice is the lion and she found comfort and strength in viewing the bronze winged lion sculpture at Piazza San Marco.

Just as the lion gave Chanel the strength to carry on, she chose to incorporate it into her surroundings. Two lions were positioned on her dining room table at her apartment on Rue Cambon, a heavy golden lion with a raised paw was displayed on the living room mantelpiece and above her desk was a framed painting of a lion. She also carried the lion into her designs – the buttons of the famous Chanel jacket are engraved with the image of the beast and golden brooches are emblazoned with a lion's head.

The House of Chanel has consistently returned to the imagery of the lion in honour of the designer. In 2010, a huge lion statue was placed at the Grand Palais in Paris, to showcase Karl Lagerfeld's collection in tribute to the 'sign of the lion', while jewellery collections since have featured diamond-encrusted lions on pendants and rings.

→ In 2010, a huge lion statue was placed at the Grand Palais in Paris, to showcase Karl Lagerfeld's collection in tribute to the 'sign of the lion'.

Create a **Timeless Signature** Accessory

In February 1955, Chanel revealed her quilted handbag with shoulder strap. She gave it the name 2.55 after its launch date. Again, numbers were used symbolically, the two and five being particularly significant to the designer. The special features of the bag acted as codes to Chanel's past, almost offering the wearer access to her secrets.

The bag was made from soft leather, hand-stitched with a diagonal pattern to create a quilted effect, known as matelassé. This recalled the jackets of the stable boys she spent time with at Royallieu, when she rode horseback and visited the racetrack with Étienne Balsan. It was yet another example of the masculine wardrobe shaping the aesthetic of her designs.

The shoulder strap to the bag consisted of a gold-plated chain with a leather cord, like that of a horse's harness. As well as being reminiscent of the key chains that dangled from the keepers of the convent at Aubazine, it was a functional detail to make life easier for women.

'I got fed up with holding my purses in my hands and losing them, so I added a strap and carried them over my shoulder,' she said. This metal chain would later be used as a detail in other aspects of Chanel designs after her death – as jewellery, belts and as detailing on haute couture. 'I know women,' she once said. 'Give them chains. Women adore chains.'

The 2.55 bag's flap was secured by a rectangular lock, originally known as 'the Mademoiselle lock', in reference to Chanel never marrying. It was updated to a clasp with the double C logo. The lining was in red, one of Chanel's key colours, supposedly chosen to make it easier to find items without having to rummage around inside.

The 2.55 bag was an instant classic, becoming the essential style statement for stars like Brigitte Bardot and Jane Fonda. Mia Farrow, another rising star of New Hollywood in the 1960s, carried with her the Chanel 2.55 while making the classic horror film *Rosemary's Baby*.

↑ The Chanel 2.55 quilted bag has become a staple accessory for street style and fashion influencers.

"I know women …
Give them chains.
Women adore chains."

Chanel

While some versions have been tweaked over the years, the bag has remained constant. Originally produced in Chanel's favourite colours of navy, beige, black and brown, a rainbow of colours were later introduced, along with experiments in different textiles and strap styles.

Chanel also used the quilted technique for jacket linings, as it was comforting and supple and was reminiscent of the equestrian spirit and healthy outdoor pursuits. The House of Chanel adopted the look of matelassé in different materials, such as in precious metals for rings, necklaces and belts and for quilted leather jackets.

← While the quilting effect was first created by Chanel for the 2.55 handbag in 1955, matelassé has been used to dramatic effect for coats, including this glimmering gold version at the Chanel Métiers d'Art show at Le Grand Palais in 2019.

Glossary

2.55 bag – The classic Chanel quilted handbag with strap, named after its launch date of February 1955.

Adrienne – Chanel's aunt Adrienne was only a year older than her, and the two worked as seamstresses together in the military town of Moulins. *See Antoinette, Jeanne.*

Antoinette – The younger sister of Coco Chanel. She was hired as a model and shop assistant for Chanel's Paris and Deauville boutiques alongside Adrienne, but tragically died in 1920 in Argentina. *See Adrienne, Jeanne.*

Art Deco – The design movement that shaped the modernism of the 1920s, and which was evident in the geometry and streamlined silhouette of Chanel's designs.

Arthur Capel – Also known as 'Boy', he was Chanel's rich half-English, half-French playboy lover, who supported her when she first founded her business. He was killed in a car crash in December 1919 in the South of France. *See Boy.*

Aubazine Abbey – Chanel and her two sisters were abandoned by their father at the convent in Aubazine, in the remote Auvergne region, after their mother died in 1895.

Avant-garde – New and experimental ideas and methods.

Ballets Russes – The Parisian-based ballet company founded by Russian Sergei Diaghilev, and which put on exotic and avant-garde performances from 1909 to 1929.

Bel Respiro – Chanel's villa in Garches, on the outskirts of Paris, which she bought in 1920 as a refugee after Boy Capel was killed. It was here that Igor Stravinsky and his family lived with Chanel for a time.

Belle Époque – Translated as 'beautiful era', the period of French history from 1871 to the outbreak of the First World War in 1914, defined by its carefree and decadent way of life.

Biarritz – The ritzy resort on the Atlantic coast of France, close to the Spanish border, where Chanel opened a boutique in 1915.

Bijoux de Diamants – Chanel's first diamond collection in 1932, featuring adaptable pieces that took inspiration from celestial imagery.

Bois des Iles – Meaning 'Island Wood', the perfume was launched in 1926, and created with Ernest Beaux to be the first woody fragrance for women.

Boy – Perfume, which transcends gender, devised by Olivier Poige in 2016. Inspired by Arthur Capel's nickname. The love of Chanel's life, he was key to the origin of the House of Chanel. *See also Arthur Capel.*

Byzantine – A style of Eastern art and architecture in the Middle Ages, centred on Constantinople (modern-day Istanbul), which was defined by religious iconography, gold decoration and geometric mosaic designs.

Camellia – The white, scentless flower which became the symbol of the Chanel brand. *See Chanel Nº5; Gardénia.*

Cécile Sorel – A French comedic actress of the Belle Époque, known for her extravagant stage costumes and an early customer of Chanel's.

Chanel Nº5 – The first perfume created by Coco Chanel, becoming one of the best-selling of all time following its launch in 1921. *See Camellia and Gardénia.*

Coco – The nickname of Gabrielle Chanel, believed to have originated from her time as a singer in the café-concerts of Moulins, belting out the song *'Qui qu'a vu Coco' and 'Ko Ko Ri Ko'.*

Coromandel screens – A lacquered Chinese folding screen decorated with intricate designs, and first imported from China in the seventeenth century via India's Coromandel coast. It was a favourite object of Chanel's, featured in her apartment and boutique on Rue Cambon.

Cuir de Russie – A fragrance released by Chanel and Ernest Beaux in 1927, with a name inspired by the exiled Russian aristocrats in Paris in the 1920s, including her lover, Grand Duke Dmitri Pavlovich.

Deauville – The fashionable Belle Époque beach resort on the Normandy coast was famed for its racecourse and casino; it was where Chanel opened a boutique in 1913.

Dmitri Pavlovich – the Grand Duke was Chanel's lover in the twenties. He was the first cousin of Tsar Nicholas II and fled Russia in 1917 after his involvement in the assassination of Rasputin.

Duke of Westminster – Hugh Grosvenor, the Second Duke of Westminster, was considered one of the richest men in Europe when he dated Chanel from 1924 until 1930.

Émilienne d'Alençon – The celebrity courtesan, actress and dancer of the Folies Bergère was the mistress of Étienne Balsan and his guest at Royallieu. She was the first client of Coco Chanel, after admiring her simple hats.

Ernest Beaux – The Russian perfumer who worked with Chanel to create her original perfumes, beginning with Chanel Nº5 from his workshop in Grasse, in the South of France.

Étienne Balsan – The wealthy polo player and horse racer who invited Chanel to his chateau Royallieu, near Compiègne. They originally met in Moulins, when he was stationed there as a cavalry officer, and he helped to fund her early hat business.

Flying Cloud – The luxury yacht owned by the Duke of Westminster, which featured gleaming white sails.

Garçonne – Taking its name from the 1922 novel by Victor Margueritte, the term described a sexually liberated young woman who lived her life freely. The *garçonne* style was defined by loose, freedom-giving clothing.

Gardénia – Named after the white flower, a favourite of Chanel's, the floral perfume created with Ernest Beaux, was launched in 1925. *See Chanel Nº5, Camellia.*

Genre pauvre – Literally means 'poor look', the style that Chanel popularized, putting women in workmen's clothes, a waitress's white collar and cuffs, a ditch digger's scarf. *See also poverty de luxe.*

Gripoix – A Parisian jewellery company founded by Augustine Gripoix in 1869, specialising in costume jewellery techniques. Chanel teamed up with Maison Gripoix in 1924 for her first jewellery collection.

Jersey fabric – A soft and supple fabric originally used for men's underwear, and adapted by Chanel for her first collections around 1913. It became the signature of the Chanel look.

Jean Cocteau – The avant-garde French writer, artist and filmmaker was a close friend of Chanel's, and the two collaborated on numerous projects from the 1920s onwards.

Jeanne – Chanel's mother, Jeanne Devolle, married Albert Chanel in 1884, and they had five children together. She died in Brive-la-Gaillarde of tuberculosis in 1895, at the age of thirty-three.

Julia-Bertha – the older sister of Chanel, she died in 1913, leaving behind a son, Andre, who Chanel cared for.

Karl Lagerfeld – The French couturier who was appointed creative director of the House of Chanel in 1983, until his death in 2019.

La Pausa – Chanel's luxury villa on the Roquebrune-Cap-Martin peninsula, between Monte Carlo and the Italian border. Built in 1929, it was inspired by the Provençal style of the region and the architecture of Aubazine Abbey.

Lion – One of Chanel's beloved symbols, inspired by the sign of the zodiac Leo, Chanel's birth sign. Also, the emblem of the city of Venice.

Little Black Dress (LBD) – One of the signature looks of Chanel, a simple black sheath was given the name Little Black Dress by *Vogue* in 1926.

Mademoiselle – Coco Chanel was addressed as Mademoiselle by those who worked for her, and as a woman who never married, she embraced the title as a representation of her independence.

Marthe Davelli – The famed French soprano and friend and customer of Coco Chanel's, who she is believed to have first met in Biarritz in 1915.

Matelassé – the stitching technique to create a quilting effect, which Chanel used for her leather 2.55 handbag. The quilting pattern is also used for Chanel's coats and engraved in jewellery.

Misia Sert – the Polish-born artist's muse and patron who hosted a popular salon in Paris. She was one of Chanel's closest friends, introducing her to avant-garde artists and writers.

Modernism – A movement of the early twentieth century which was characterised by new forms of expression to represent the experiences of modern industrial life.

Monte Carlo – The Monaco playground of the rich and famous, noted for its casino, where Chanel met the Duke of Westminster at Christmas 1923 and Hollywood mogul Samuel Goldwyn in 1929.

Moulins – The former military town in the Allier department of France, where Chanel worked as a seamstress and a singer after leaving Aubazine Abbey. It was here she first met Étienne Balsan.

Pau – The town in the Pyrenees where Étienne Balsan owned a home and played polo. It was here that Chanel is believed to have first met Boy Capel. *See Arthur Capel; Boy*.

Place Vendôme – The grand octagonal square in the 1st arrondissement of Paris, where the Ritz Hotel is located. This was home to Chanel for decades.

Poverty de luxe – Coined by contemporary Paul Poiret, a dig at Chanel's *genre pauvre*, her unadorned garments, an expensive interpretation of a more simple style usually made with more modest fabrics. *See genre pauvre*.

Pyjamas – Not just for nightwear, the term described loose trousers in the 1920s and 30s, which could be worn on the beach or as evening dress.

Rosehall – The home in the Scottish Highlands where Chanel lived with the Duke of Westminster in the late 1920s, and decorated in her style.

Roquebrune-Cap-Martin – Situated between Monaco and Menton, on the French Riviera, it is the location of Chanel's villa, La Pausa, built in 1929.

Royallieu – The château and former abbey owned by Étienne Balsan, and located in the Compiègne forest, where Chanel lived from around 1905 until 1909.

Rue Cambon – the narrow street behind Place Vendôme, in the fashion district of Paris, where Chanel opened her original boutique in 1910. She bought 31 Rue Cambon in 1919 for her salon, apartment and workrooms, and it is still the home of Chanel.

Saumur – This medieval town, situated on the Loire River, was the birthplace of Coco Chanel in 1883.

Stravinsky – The Russian composer of avant-garde works included the controversial *The Rite of Spring*. He was Chanel's lover for a period of time and stayed with her at Bel Respiro. He was one of the inspirations for her Russian collection in the 1920s.

Suzanne Orlandi – A French actress and courtesan who was one of Chanel's early clients, after meeting at Royallieu.

Tricots Chanel – The textile factory opened by Chanel in the early 1920s, and located in Asnières-sur-Seine. The name was changed to Tissus Chanel in 1929, when she expanded into silks and tweeds.

Tweed jacket – The signature look of Coco Chanel, the tweed jacket was initially inspired by the British aristocrats she met in the 1920s.

Venice – A favourite city of Chanel's, she admired the beauty of the Byzantine architecture and Renaissance art, the beach at the Lido and the lion symbol of the city. *See Lion*.

Virginie Viard – A French fashion designer and creative director of the House of Chanel since 2019, following the death of Karl Lagerfeld.

Vogue – The quintessential fashion magazine and style bible, first published in New York City in 1892.

Wheat – A symbol of prosperity, Chanel chose to display sheaths of wheat in her apartment, or depicted in bronze and crystal.

Picture Credits

The publishers would like to thank all those listed below for permission to reproduce the images. Every care has been taken to trace copyright holders. Any copyright holders we have been unable to reach are invited to contact the publishers so that a full acknowledgement may be given in subsequent editions.

Alamy: 17, 37 (Granger Historical Picture Archive).

Bridgeman: 85 (©Tallandier / Bridgeman Images).

Getty: 13 (Guy Marineau); 14 (Gianni Penati); 18, 50 (Daniel Simon); 21 (Edward Steichen); 23, 56, 132 l (Victor Virgile); 24 r; 24 l, 109, 138 (Kristy Sparow); 27 (Paul Schutzer); 28, 123 l (Pierre Verdy); 29 (Matthew Sperzel); 31 (New York Times Co); 35, 80 (Thierry Orban); 39, 49, 60 (Peter White); 40, 99 (Pascal Le Segretain); 47 (Gerard Julien); 51, 104 (Douglas Kirkland); 55 (Pietro D'Aprano); 59 (Historical Picture Archive); 63 (Jean-Pierre Muller); 65 (Mondadori Portfolio); 69, 111 (Mike Marsland); 71 (Sasha); 73, 79 (Horst P/. Horst); 75 (Eugene Robert Richee); 77, 87 (Time Life Pictures); 83 (Vittorio Zunino Celotto); 84 (Edward Berthelot); 89 (Pierre Vauthey); 91 (Alex Quinio); 92 (Michael Ochs Archive); 95 (Habans Patrice); 100, 131 (Charles Sheeler); 101 (Robert Doisneau); 103 (Tim Graham); 107 (Stephane Cardinale); 113 (Estrop); 119 (Cooper Neill); 121 (Adoc-photos); 125 (Antonio de Moraes Barros Filho); 127 (Rindoff/Charriau); 129 (Francois Durand); 132 r (Dominique Charriau); 137 (Daniel Zuchnik).

Rex: 32 (Christophe Petit Tesson/ EPA-EFE/Shutterstock); 43 (Hatami/Shutterstock); 45, 114, 117 (Granger/Shutterstock); 76 (Goldwyn/United Artists/Kobal/ Shutterstock); 123 (Steve Wood/ Shutterstock); 135 (Shutterstock).

Tokyo Fashion: 66 ©Kira / TokyoFashion.com.

Index

accessories 42–45, 134–135
Alençon, Émilienne d' 56–57, 139
Aristotle 104
Arnaud, Marie-Hélène 88
Art Deco 18, 19, 20, 34, 39, 45, 124, 138
Aubazine Abbey 4, 5, 7, 36, 39,
  52–55, 104, 114, 132, 134, 138

Bacall, Lauren 91
bags 5, 7, 10, 42–43, 45, 47,
  91, 104, 134–137, 138
Ballet Russes 7, 70, 76, 106, 138
Balsan, Étienne 6, 10, 56,
  66, 134, 139, 140
Bardot, Brigitte 7, 91, 110, 134
beading 40, 106, 124, 131
Beaux, Ernest 45, 104, 138, 139
beige 7, 36–37, 38, 39, 52
belts 15, 23, 42, 47, 54, 134
Bernhardt, Sarah 128
Biarritz 34, 36, 76, 96, 106, 138
bias cut 32, 118
Blondell, Joan 74
Bohan, Marc 93
braiding 36
Breton top 5, 7, 13, 14, 80–81, 110–113
Brooks, Louise 72–73
buttons 24, 36, 131, 132

camellia 15, 24, 26, 128–131, 138
Capel, Boy 6–7, 10, 34, 60, 62, 66,
  83, 84, 96, 104, 114, 132, 138

cardigan 40, 80, 82–83, 113
cardigan jacket 16, 17, 24, 48, 69
Cardin, Pierre 93
chain details 36–37, 42–43,
  45, 54, 122, 134
Chanel, Coco
  life 4, 5–7
  name 6, 104, 139
  public persona 60–61
Chanel brand 6
Chanel logo 7, 24, 34, 52, 104, 134
Chanel Look 24–25, 48, 72–73
Claire, Ina 2, 74, 131
Cocteau, Jean 70, 139
collars 23, 53, 56
colour 36–41, 52, 79, 83, 86–87, 96, 134
comfort 6, 7, 10, 13, 18,
  24–25, 26, 40, 62, 118
consistency 46–49
coromandel screens 76, 106,
  124, 139
Courrèges, André 46
crepe de Chine 20, 40, 76, 92, 106
Cubism 18, 70
culottes 12, 13

Dalí, Salvador 71
Davelli, Marthe 140
Deauville 4, 6, 7, 10, 15, 16,
  60, 80–81, 110, 139
Deneuve, Catherine 88, 91
Diaghilev, Sergei 7, 70, 76, 106, 138

Dietrich, Marlene 13, 72
Dior, Christian 5, 24, 65, 92, 93, 118
disregarding the rules 5

elegance 46, 124
embroidery 7, 13, 20, 40, 76, 78,
  106–109, 126–127, 130–131
Evans, Madge 74

Fair Isle tricot 40
Farrow, Mia 134
Ferguson Brothers 40
film costumes 70, 72–74, 88–91
Fonda, Jane 91, 134
freedom of movement 7, 13,
  18, 24, 46, 62, 92, 118, 124

Garbo, Greta 72, 74
garçonne **look** 5, 6, 10, 18,
  32, 36, 110, 118, 139
gardénia 45, 139
gendered dress 5
genre pauvre 14–17, 34, 139
gold 36–37, 136
  buttons 24, 36
grey 36
Gripoix, Augustine 122, 139

hairstyle 5, 18, 28–29, 60, 68, 72–73
hats 6, 10, 14, 16, 24, 42–43, 56, 80
Hepburn, Audrey 110
Hepburn, Katharine 13, 72

jackets 6, 10, 91
  cardigan 16, 17, 24, 48, 69
  linings 24, 26, 39, 102, 137
  tweed 24–27, 34, 39, 40,
    66–69, 100–102, 140
jersey fabric 6, 14–17, 20, 36, 40, 60,
  66, 80, 92, 96–99, 106, 113, 139
jewellery 7, 42–45, 52, 122–123
  chain details 36–37,
    42–43, 45, 122, 134
  cuff bracelets 43, 47, 52, 54, 87, 122
  diamonds 114–115, 138
  pearls 5, 23, 34, 43, 72–73,
    76, 118, 122–123
jodhpurs 6, 10

Kelly, Grace 91
Kennedy, Jackie 7, 91
Kitmir 109
Klein, Bernat 102

La Pausa 86, 112, 114–115, 139
lace 7, 32–33, 40, 118–119, 124, 129
Lagerfeld, Karl 7, 139
Les Six 70
lingerie, elements from 32–33
linings 24, 26, 39, 102, 137
Linton, William 40, 100, 102
lion motif 24, 83, 104,
  114, 132–133, 139
lipstick 39
Little Black Dress 4, 5, 7,
  20–22, 34, 46–47, 92, 140

Malle, Louis 89, 90
Maltese cross 11, 43, 52, 54, 114, 122
masculine aesthetic 5, 6, 10–13,
  24, 34, 45, 66–69, 72
matelassé 5, 7, 10, 45, 47,
  134–137, 140
metallic textiles 13, 32, 40
minimalism 20
modernism 33, 70, 76, 124, 140
monochrome 5, 7, 17, 20–23,
  28–35, 52–53, 110
Monroe, Marilyn 90
Moreau, Jeanne 7, 89, 91
Murphy, Gerald 110

Naval style 7, 80–83, 110–113
numbers 104–105, 114

Orlandi, Suzanne 56, 140

Paris shop 4, 6, 35, 59, 62
Parker, Suzy 7, 88
Pavlovich, Grand Duke Dmitri
  66, 106, 122, 139
Pavlovna, Grand Duchess Maria
  109
pearls 5, 23, 34, 43, 72–73,
  76, 118, 122–123, 126
perfumes 7
  Bois des Iles 45, 138
  Boy 138
  Chanel No5 4, 5, 18, 45,
    83, 84, 91, 104, 139
  Chanel No22 45, 104
  Cuir de Russie 45, 66, 139
  Gardénia 45
Picasso, Pablo 70, 110
pioneering fashion vocabulary 5
pockets 13, 14, 15, 16, 24
Poiret, Paul 23, 42, 92
polo sweaters 10, 66
poverty de luxe 14–17, 34, 140
printed fabrics 7, 32
pyjamas 7, 13, 28–29, 48,
  74, 80, 84–85, 140

quilting See matelassé

Rabanne, Paco 46
red 38–39, 134
Renoir, Jean 70
resort style 80–81
Reverdy, Pierre 70, 91
Rodier, Jean 96
Russian collection 66, 76, 78, 109
Russian emigrés 7, 66, 76, 109, 139

sailor collars 80, 113
Saint Laurent, Yves 13, 46, 93, 140
Schneider, Romy 88
Seberg, Jean 110
sequins 7, 106, 124–125, 127, 135
Sert, Misia 70, 83, 140
Seyrig, Delphine 91
shirt-waister dresses 23
shoes 42
  cork-soled sandals 85, 86
  two-tone 39, 42, 91
shoulder bags 134

simplicity 6, 10, 13, 14, 17,
  20, 45, 52–55, 62, 65
skirts
  length 13, 19, 24, 32, 93, 118
  pleated 18, 40, 69, 80, 83, 113
Sorel, Cécile 62, 139
star motif 114–117
Stravinsky, Igor 66, 70, 76, 140
stripes 110–113
  Breton top 5, 7, 13, 14, 80–81, 110–113
style, endurance 5
suits 7, 46, 91
  culotte 12, 13
  trouser 11, 13, 34, 127
  tweed 11, 13, 24–27, 32, 100–102, 127
  Watteau 78
Swanson, Gloria 75

tanned skin 5, 19, 28, 30, 84–85
Taylor, Elizabeth 91
theatre and ballet costumes 70–71
theosophy 114
Tricots Chanel 40, 140
trousers 6, 10, 11, 13, 34, 112, 127
  pyjamas 7, 13, 28–29, 48,
    74, 80, 84–85, 140
Truffaut, François 70, 91
tulle 7, 20, 21, 32, 36, 40
tunic 12–13, 17
turtlenecks 66, 80
tweed 5, 7, 10, 11, 13, 24–27, 32,
  40–41, 66–69, 100–102, 127, 140
  bouclé 100–102

Vadim, Roger 70
velvet 20, 23, 32, 38–39, 56,
  76–78, 86–87, 106, 124
Venice 81, 83–86, 132, 140
Verdura, Fulco di 43, 122
Viard, Virginie 7, 140
Visconti, Luchino 70, 88

waistline 6, 10, 32, 60, 98, 118, 120
Wales, Princess of 101
Watteau collection 77, 78
Westminster, Duke of 59, 60, 66–67,
  69, 80, 100, 113, 122, 139, 140
wheat motif 107, 140
white satin 28–30

zeitgeist 18, 62–65

First published in 2021 by
Frances Lincoln Publishing
an imprint of The Quarto Group.
The Old Brewery, 6 Blundell Street
London, N7 9BH,
United Kingdom
T (0)20 7700 6700
www.QuartoKnows.com

A catalogue record for this book is
available from the British Library.

ISBN 978 0 7112 5909 6
Ebook ISBN 978 0 7112 5910 2

10 9 8 7 6 5 4 3 2

Design by Intercity

Printed in China